*"Cancer: Nurturing Self Guides has been such a [gift?]. This book is a gift that keeps on giving* [...] *and easy, and several messages stuck with me: the ones that I needed to hear at this point in Life. However, I plan to keep this book close by, and open a page at random, for a quick reconnection with Spirit and guidance, or choose a chapter to inspire needed change in that area of Life.*

*The channeled wisdom and messages are practically organized and cover all the most important Life aspects: from self-love and relationships, through home, health, work, and spirituality, to creativity and fulfillment, and even Birthday messages! The intro guides readers of all astrology knowledge levels on how to best make use of the messages depending on where the Cancer sign is located in their natal chart (sun sign, ascendent, moon, North node, etc..). A wide range of spirit guides are introduced, and each one of them brings their unique wisdom, flavor, and perspective and connects the reader to a specific natural or spiritual element.*

*This book increased my acceptance and appreciation of how my Cancer rising sign influences my character and needs, and, most of all, it gave me tools on how to make the most of its strength, and tips on how to bring about more balance while remaining aligned to my truth. In particular, I deeply resonated with how important it is to cultivate an inner sense of safety/home and to allow myself to go through the waves of emotions without being overwhelmed by them, and how these two practices reinforce each other. I've also gained clarity on my need to please and nourish others, how to balance it with self-care, and why I can benefit by being more selective about who I give my caring attention to.*

*I definitely recommend this book to those seeking guidance and inspiration on how to rise to the best version of themselves and shine their own unique light."*

**-Joy Irene Stefani of Joy Life Coaching, Cancer Rising Sign**

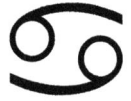

# CANCER

## NURTURING SENTIMENTS

### FROM YOUR SIGN'S SPIRIT GUIDES

WRITTEN AND CHANNELED BY

# ANNA SWANSUN

Copyright © 2023 by Anna Swansun

Exton, PA: SWANSUN LLC

Cover Design by Anna Swansun

All rights reserved. No portion of this book may be reproduced by any mechanical, photographic, or electronic process, or in the form of recording; nor may it be stored in a retrieval system, transmitted, or otherwise copied for public or private use—other than for "fair use" as brief quotations embodied in articles and review—without prior permission of the publisher. Contact information: hello@annaswansun.com

The author of this book does not dispense medical advice or prescribe the use of any technique as a form of treatment for physical, mental, emotional, or medical problems. The author and publisher encourage you to seek professional medical advice, insight, and assistance for any and all ailments or questions, physical, psychological, financial, or otherwise. The intention of the author is only to offer general information to assist you in your spiritual path. In the event you use any of the information in this book for yourself, the author and publisher assume no responsibility for your actions.

ISBN: 979-8366057745

# TO ♋

*With an Unfathomable Urge to Nurture
and a Deep-Seated Aquifer of Tenacity
when Aligned and Self-Assured
You Are an Oasis of Tranquility*

Joy—
Thank you so much for writing such a heartfelt review. I appreciate it. You are such a kind and beautiful person. Trust in your amazing intuitive abilities and keep sharing your light! ♡ Much love & Mystical Blessings!

Anna Swanson

# CONTENTS

## WHERE IT ALL STARTS  0

About Cancer Signs .........................................................1
The Purpose....................................................................5
How I Connect with Your Guides ..................................8

## MEET YOUR SPIRIT GUIDES  11

Your Spirit Animal: Crab .............................................13
Your Crystal Guide: Lapis Lazuli................................16
Your Ascended Master: Isis.........................................19
Your Rune: Ansuz – Ancestor Messages................23
Your Nature Spirit Guides: Nymphs .......................26
Your Archangel Guide: Archangel Lavender..........28
Your Herb Guide: Yarrow...........................................31
Your Tarot Guide: Page of Pentacles.......................34
Your Tree: Oak..............................................................37
Your Ruling Planet: The Moon.................................40

## WORK | BUSINESS  45

Crab ...............................................................................47

Lapis Lazuli ................................................................ 48
Isis ............................................................................ 49
Ansuz - Anna's Ancestor Guides ........................... 50
Nymphs .................................................................... 51
Archangel Lavender................................................. 52
Yarrow ...................................................................... 54
Page of Pentacles .................................................... 55
Oak............................................................................ 56
Moon......................................................................... 57
Most Treasured Takeaways ..................................... 58

# WEALTH | ABUNDANCE     61

Crab........................................................................... 63
Lapis Lazuli ............................................................... 64
Isis ............................................................................ 65
Ansuz – Anna's Ancestor Guides ........................... 66
Nymphs .................................................................... 67
Archangel Lavender................................................. 68
Yarrow ...................................................................... 69
Page of Pentacles .................................................... 70
Oak............................................................................ 71
Moon......................................................................... 72
Most Treasured Takeaways ..................................... 73

# LOVE 77

Crab .................................................................. 79
Lapis Lazuli ..................................................... 83
Isis .................................................................... 84
Ansuz – Anna's Ancestor Guides .............................. 87
Nymphs ............................................................ 88
Archangel Lavender ........................................ 89
Yarrow .............................................................. 91
Page of Pentacles ............................................ 92
Oak .................................................................... 93
Moon ................................................................ 94
Most Treasured Takeaways ............................ 95

# FRIENDS | FAMILY 99

Crab .................................................................. 101
Lapis Lazuli ..................................................... 102
Isis .................................................................... 103
Ansuz - Anna's Ancestor Guides .............................. 104
Nymphs ............................................................ 105
Archangel Lavender ........................................ 106
Yarrow .............................................................. 107
Page of Pentacles ............................................ 109
Oak .................................................................... 110
Moon ................................................................ 111

Most Treasured Takeaways ..................................... 112

## FUN | HAPPINESS  115

Crab ............................................................................. 117
Lapis Lazuli ................................................................ 118
Isis ............................................................................... 119
Ansuz - Anna's Ancestor Guides ........................... 120
Nymphs ...................................................................... 121
Archangel Lavender .................................................. 122
Yarrow ........................................................................ 123
Page of Pentacles ...................................................... 124
Oak .............................................................................. 125
Moon ........................................................................... 126
Most Treasured Takeaways ..................................... 127

## HOME  131

Crab ............................................................................. 133
Lapis Lazuli ................................................................ 134
Isis ............................................................................... 135
Ansuz – Anna's Ancestor Guides ........................... 136
Nymphs ...................................................................... 137
Archangel Lavender .................................................. 138
Yarrow ........................................................................ 140
Page of Pentacles ...................................................... 141
Oak .............................................................................. 142

Moon ..................................................................144
Most Treasured Takeaways .........................145

# WELLBEING 149

Crab ....................................................................151
Lapis Lazuli .......................................................152
Isis ......................................................................153
Ansuz - Anna's Ancestors ................................154
Nymphs .............................................................155
Archangel Lavender .........................................156
Yarrow ...............................................................157
Page of Pentacles ..............................................158
Oak .....................................................................159
Moon ..................................................................160
Most Treasured Takeaways .........................161

# SPIRITUALITY    165

Crab ....................................................................167
Lapis Lazuli .......................................................169
Isis ......................................................................170
Ansuz - Anna's Ancestors ................................172
Nymphs .............................................................173
Archangel Lavender .........................................174
Yarrow ...............................................................175
Page of Pentacles ..............................................176

Oak .................................................................. 178
Moon ................................................................ 179
Most Treasured Takeaways ................................. 180

## CREATIVITY 183

Crab ................................................................. 185
Lapis Lazuli .................................................... 186
Isis ................................................................... 187
Ansuz - Anna's Ancestor Guides ......................... 188
Nymphs ........................................................... 189
Archangel Lavender .......................................... 190
Yarrow ............................................................. 191
page of Pentacles .............................................. 192
Oak .................................................................. 193
Moon ................................................................ 194
Most Treasured Takeaways ................................. 195

## BIRTHDAY MESSAGES  199

Crab ................................................................. 201
Lapis Lazuli .................................................... 202
Isis ................................................................... 203
Ansuz - Anna's Ancestor Guides ......................... 204
Nymphs ........................................................... 205
Archangel Lavender .......................................... 206
Yarrow ............................................................. 207

Page of Pentacles ........................................................ 208
Oak ............................................................................ 209
Moon .......................................................................... 210
Most Treasured Takeaways ...................................... 211

# AND WHERE IT REALLY BEGINS ... 215

Conclusion ................................................................ 217
Resources .................................................................. 219
References & Further Reading ............................... 222
Acknowledgements .................................................. 224
More About Anna Swansun ................................... 226

# WHERE IT ALL STARTS

## ABOUT CANCER[1] SIGNS

You, caring ♋ soul, create a wave of sustenance, attentiveness, care, and soothing wherever you are! With nourishment, intuition, and parental-like affection you accept your watery existence with emotional recovery!

I love ♋ people and adore the reassurance and care they demonstrate whatever space you they in!

Whether your Sun illuminates ♋, your Moon resides in ♋, or you were born as a ♋ ascendent (rising), this book celebrates your truth and manifests as a Great Mother guide for you.[2] If the sign of ♋ holds your north node, this book serves as your compass If you are supplemented with a stellium (a cluster of three or more planets in a single sign or house) in the sign of ♋, this

---

[1] I believe that words are extremely powerful. Unfortunately, your sign's name has another meaning associated with disease, illness, and unhealthy cells. Because the word is most often used to represent the disease, it is natural for us to associate the word with that first even though in the context of astrology, we know it to be the fourth sign of the zodiac. So, I am instead replacing the plethora of times I would write the word 'cancer' with your sign's glyph, ♋. Symbols, too, are significantly powerful, and this symbol directly links to your essence as the fourth astrological sign, so it may feel even more innately connected to your soul than the word does.

[2] If your sun, moon or ascendent is at 27, 28 or 29 degrees of Gemini, you were born on the cusp of ♋ and presumably embody traits of Gemini as well as ♋ characteristics. Likewise, if they are at 27, 28, or 29 degrees of ♋, you are likely blessed with many characteristics of both ♋ and Leo.

# WHERE IT ALL STARTS

book centers your nourishing blessings and encourages necessary balance.

Let's explore a bit more about what these signs and configurations represent. I have seen numerous interpretations of sun, moon, and rising signs from different astrologers. Allow me to explain what I have gathered.

The sun sign represents how you show up in the world. This depicts how others see you, your outward personality. The Sun brings each of us light, joy, and life, so living in alignment with your sun sign will help you find your vitality and happiness. Imagine a cloudy, stormy day. We all have them, a day when you are feeling under the weather, down, damp or a bit brain fogged. If you are feeling blue and you want to feel more warmth, lightness, or sunshine, do what your sun sign exudes. Whether it is a cloudy day, a rainy week or even a storm-filled year, living like your Sun will help you roll the clouds away.[3] So, if your Sun enlightens ♋, following the encouraging advice in this book will help you to clarify your personality and embody more of your light!

The Moon symbolizes feelings and emotions, often described as being the sensitive part of us that our nearest and dearest know us to be. As your celestial mother, your Moon soothes and nurtures you. She comforts you in the darkness and illuminates your unconscious through dreams and cycles of patterning. So, if your Moon lives in

---

[3] Michael Lutin repetitively iterates this teaching to emphasize the important of our sun signs and the house our sun resides in.

♋

♋, these messages will be comforting and nourishing, while giving you emotionally intelligent advice to feel safer and more in tune with your natural state. The moon inhabits her home sign when in ♋, so you may feel her tides affect you more than others. Inviting her to assist you as you move through emotional phases will be extremely impactful for you.

The ascendent, or rising sign, signifies your true self. This sign exhibits the opportunity for more alignment to make karmic resolutions, tap into the soul, and fulfill destiny. The ascendent just is, whether you want it to be or not. It epitomizes you, and although I believe the entire chart exists as a map for your life, the ascendent sign provides the tools you need to navigate it. If you were born with ♋ as your ascendent, the nurturing sentiments in this book will help you to align with who you truly are and augment your life purpose.

The north node acts as your compass rose. It gives you direction throughout your entire life. As something you ought to learn about in this lifetime, following it may not necessarily be comfortable, but it expands you for growth, abundance, and rich fulfillment. With a ♋ north node, follow these messages for your life's heading!

With a stellium (three or more planets in one sign or four plus if the sun or moon are included) in ♋ you reflect an eminence of flowing water energy! All ♋ sign traits will be dilated! —both positive and negative. Any stellium may cause a person to become a bit imbalanced, and with one in ♋, developing emotional intelligence, avoiding overwhelm, and nurturing yourself first becomes an

## WHERE IT ALL STARTS

absolute necessity. On the other hand, wow! You are a fountain of affection with the motherload of potential to empathize with those who need to heal their inner child and live an emotionally opulent life. These messages will encourage you to fill your cup fully to overflow your innate nourishment with the whole world!

In order to find out your sun, moon and rising signs, locate your north node, or determine if you have a stellium, go to a website such as astro.com or astrologycafe.com where you can find a free natal chart and description. You will need your birth date, time, and location. I created a video tutorial found at
 https://www.annaswansun.com/findyoursign  where you can learn how to read your chart and determine your signs.

To get messages for each of your signs go to annaswansun.com to preview or purchase those books too!

## THE PURPOSE

My sun illuminates the sign of Sagittarius, which behooves you to know because

> A) it explains why I provide you with a *variety* of perspectives from ten different types of spirit guides
> B) it gives you the overarching idea of why I created this book!

Allow me to explain: Sagittarius souls love to have more, of everything! That means we have an affinity for variety, but also a need for moderation and balance! I have learned several times over (often the hard way) that living in the extremes is not wise or healthy.

Each sign has its strengths and weaknesses. (I have just explained one of each for Sagittarius.) By acknowledging and accepting our weaknesses, we gain more strength. So, setting an intention for moderation and balance and following through with our actions supports the innate strengths of the signs but saves us from allowing our inherent characteristics to push us overboard or overwhelm us.

Therefore, I deliberately chose some of the guides to match ♋ sign energy, such as Crab, your constellation; Moon, your ruling planet; and Nymphs, your sign's nature spirits, and they give you encouragement and model the most pleasant facets of ♋ characteristics. Conversely, the other guides volunteered to act as your messengers to help you see from a different perspective. For instance, Oak, your tree guide, embodies unyielding strength. His

# WHERE IT ALL STARTS

messages help you create steady structures and find other ways to maintain balance. More about your guides in the next section!

I am having such a delightful time channeling these messages for you, and I know they will bring you value time and time again as often as you want to read them. During the formatting and editing process, I am reading these messages again and again, and I am gaining deeper insights and cherishing more *aha* moments upon each review.

It is important to note that some messages will resonate more than others, and it may be that you will not feel any sort of alignment with a certain message only to go back several months later or even years later to find that same message speaks to your soul in exactly the way you need. Check to make sure that the guidance is right for you. Use your internal guide, your gut feeling, and/or your higher self, and don't turn down a second opinion if you feel inclined to get one. This is not a replacement for professional help from health professionals, financial advisors, herbalists, energy workers, or any other kind of Earth angels.

Be open to exploring the messages that do align right away as you read them and pay attention to synchronicities. These are signs from spirit that reiterate or emphasize the messages you hear. For example, you may read in this book a message from Archangel Lavender and then see the color lavender pop out in several places or you will smell Lavender the herb throughout your week. That is how Spirit sometimes operates. Allow this book to not simply be a book you read once straight-through, but rather a reserve you can come back to, utilize bibliomancy[4] with, a resource you can jump around in, and an experience that helps you connect with Spirit in your own way. You found this book for a reason. Spirit is speaking to you.

All of that to say, I know you will enjoy the wisdom and peace in these spirit messages to ensure you do not get in a cycle of overwhelm, to encourage that you flow with your feelings smoothly, and to assure that you take good care of yourself before you adore and nourish the whole world with your authentic attention, balming reassurance, and ample nourishment!

For bonus content, such as meditations, more channeled messages, a downloadable Moon bookmark, and tools for augmenting your ability to outpour sustenance and avoiding overwhelm visit and register for free at
https://www.annaswansun.com/courses/cancer

---

[4] Bibliomancy is the practice of asking a question and inviting the answer to appear by using a book. Hold the question in your mind (or say it out loud)—it may be as simple as "What do I need to Know in this Moment?" Then, intuitively choose what page to open the book to. There is your answer! It is primarily used for spiritual insights, although it can be for knowing what to study, choosing a recipe, or anything else. The term originated from flipping to a page in the Bible for a daily message.

WHERE IT ALL STARTS

## HOW I CONNECT WITH YOUR GUIDES

So, where do these messages come from? I channel them. The term "to channel" has been loosely used in many places, so I want to clarify what it means to me, so you can come up with your own understanding.

My primary clair-gift is clairaudience, which means I hear (with my inner ear) messages from Spirit. I am both a medium and a channeler.

A medium hears with their inner ear the spirits at low to mid-frequency range—these spirits are humans who have not yet gone to the light (AKA ghosts), a singular animal spirit (for example: the spirit that animal communicators connect with), nature spirits (such as fairies or trees), certain guides, among others. The medium primarily works through the third-eye chakra, and either goes into a light trance to listen to the messages or goes into a full trance, in which the spirit takes over both the body and consciousness. I am a light trance medium and have full consciousness while I receive messages, a translator for non-physical.

Channeling varies slightly and instead exercises the crown chakra primarily as well as the throat and heart chakras. Channeling transmits and translates an energy sent from high vibrational spirits into words. This includes angels, Archangels, gods, goddesses, high level guides, galactic beings, and Ascended Masters. Just like with mediumship the channeler may either go into a full trance or light trance. I am also a light trance channeler, so I am fully conscious while I bring through messages from Spirit.

♋

I am so excited that you found this book and am honored to share these messages with you!

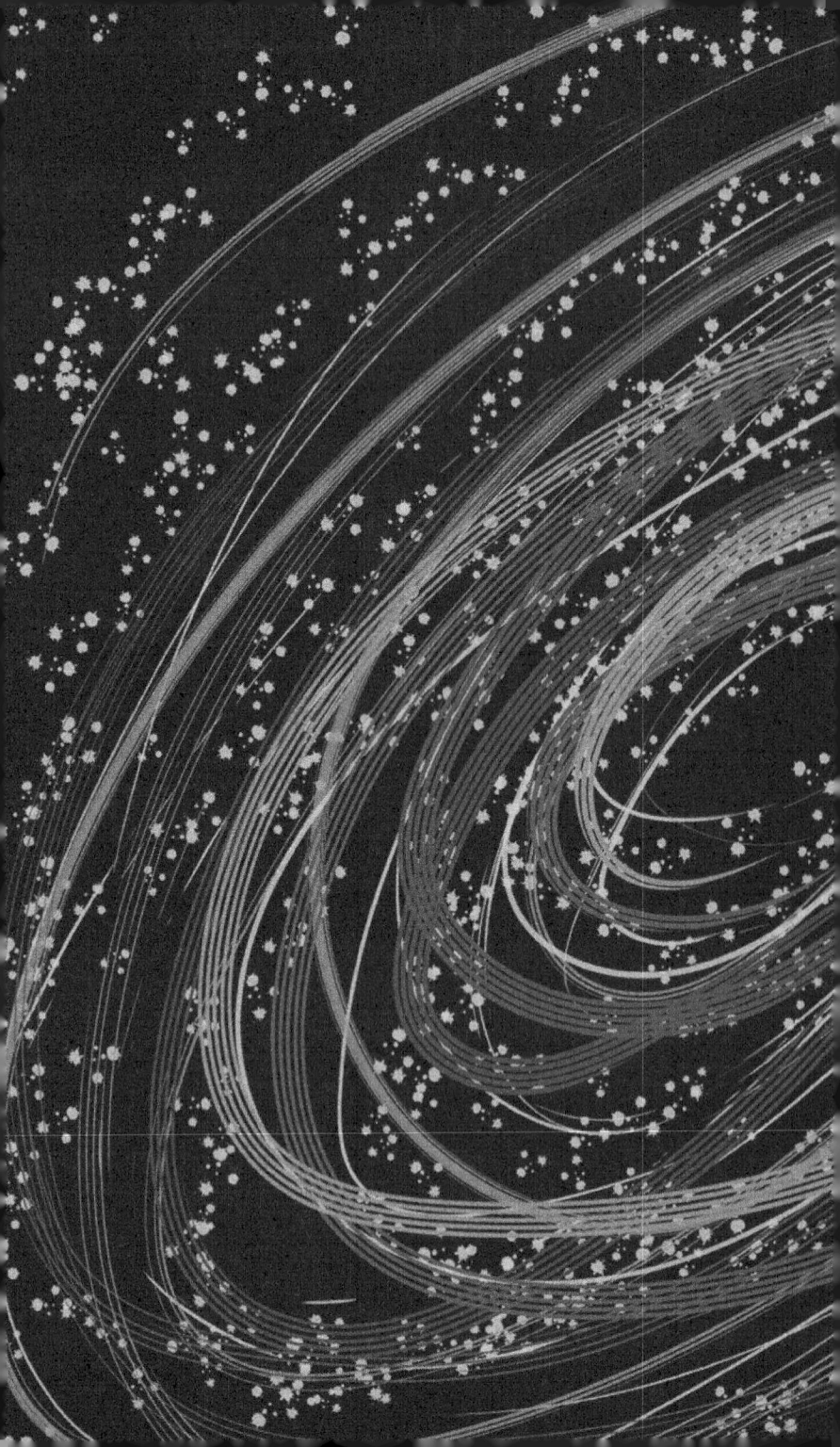

# MEET YOUR SPIRIT GUIDES

♋

## YOUR SPIRIT ANIMAL: CRAB

The constellation, or configuration of stars, of ♋ outlines the Crab.[5] She paints a picture for people with a mood of ♋ energy in their natal chart.

Crab carries her home with her, no matter where she goes. She adapts easily, as Crab lives all over the world in oceans, lakes, and even some species in trees! Crab may be very brave exploring many different areas along beaches, in volcanic lakes and even ventures as far south as Antarctica.[6] She adores being at home, but since she has figured out that it is a part of her, she can comfortably go anywhere.

She wears protective armor and maneuvers with large pinchers to defend herself. Yet, she must still be cautious because predators such as seagulls can crack through her shell with their beaks.

Often, Crab scampers across the ocean floor or burrows under the sand.

---

[5] The relationship between the constellations and signs is found in Sidereal or Vedic Astrology rather than Western Tropical Astrology. While I do use Modern Western Astrology, I still see these constellations as guides for the signs, like how Pluto (a modern planet) rules Scorpio and Mars remains the Ancient Ruler of Scorpio. Both are guides for the sign. Similarly, the Crab constellation is still a guiding force for ♋.

[6] Lori Morrison, *The Shaman's Guide to Power Animals* (Four Jaguars Press, 2019), 83.

# MEET YOUR SPIRIT GUIDES

Therefore, crab spirit animal teaches ♋ about how to be comfortable in any environment, protect their energy, and when to venture out into the world. Crab Spirit Animal asks ♋ signs to find the balance between outgoing adventures and internal alone time. Just like ♋ signs, Crab can be very sensitive and must learn how to protect herself yet be adaptable enough to venture out of her shell a bit more. Sometimes the best defense is avoiding conflict all together by learning how to flow with the emotional tides rather than allowing them to overwhelm, drag her under, or become carried away.

Crab Spirit Animal teaches ♋ when to let go and when to keep climbing.

Hear Crab Spirit Animal's Greeting:

*Listen carefully, dear ♋ signs,*
*for your world may*
*turn upside down at times.*

*Once upon a time there was a small crab,*
*barely large enough*
*to sit in the crevice of your hand,*
*and she had landed along the seashore*
*when the tide had gone out,*
*for she had been in water*
*her entire life thus far*
*and had no idea about the shore.*

♋

*She, therefore, was surprised
to find the sunshine and the blue skies.*

*You see, dear ♋ signs, some of you
have been hiding underneath the waves
your whole life and now
is the time to find the light.*

## YOUR CRYSTAL GUIDE: LAPIS LAZULI

This deep ocean-blue stone with golden flecks of pyrite and white swirls of calcite mimics the reflections of sunshine and frothy white caps on the sea. Lapis Lazuli assists ♋ to connect with their light and roll with the tides.

Lapis Lazuli is used for enhancing and protecting psychic abilities. A favorite crystal among many to use as an aid in magnifying clairvoyance, when placed atop the third eye between the eyebrows, Lapis Lazuli illuminates the inner eye. It may have been worn by the Ancient Egyptians as eyeshadow, perhaps to enhance their seer abilities.[7] The stone can also be utilized to bring prophetic dreams when placed under the pillow at night.

One of the biggest initiations for a ♋ sign soul is to work *with* their emotions rather than fight against them. Lapis Lazuli not only assists in releasing anger but also gives messages to remember how illusionary emotions can be, how fear can overtake! She suggests how to allow emotions to flow instead of becoming them and how sensitivity can be a major asset.

♋'s inclination to be highly empathetic and pick up other people's emotions is one of their biggest challenges.

Lapis Lazuli can be used as a stone to protect from psychic attack, which is essentially just other people thinking or feeling negatively towards someone else.

---

[7] Emily Anderson, *Crystals: How to Use Their Powerful Energies* (London: Sirius Publishing, 2020), 144.

Because ♋ signs are so sensitive to this, while others might not even notice, it is very important for ♋ signs to protect their energy, avoid giving too much of it away, always remember to replenish it, and overcome anxiety and worry about how others may be thinking or feeling about them.

When placed on the throat chakra, Lapis Lazuli balances. Because ♋ signs like calm, they may be peacekeepers. They can sometimes keep from saying what they feel. This causes a block in the throat chakra and can literally be felt as constriction and tightness, or perhaps a lump in the throat. If this chakra is too open, blubbering emotions well out and overwhelm all involved. The stone aids ♋ to find a happy medium.

Lapis Lazuli is an excellent resource for ♋ signs to meditate with, carry in their pocket, sleep with under their pillow, and to wear as a necklace or beaded bracelet.

Hear what Lapis Lazuli has to say:

*Hello dear ♋ signs,*
*it is nearly upon you*
*to become more aware*
*of your innate power.*

*The strength you hold is uncurable*
*in a matter of speaking,*
*for if you decide to leave it behind,*
*it will surface regardless,*

## MEET YOUR SPIRIT GUIDES

*and if you embrace it
with recognition
your senses will be heightened.*

*Therefore, learn how to use your emotions
as keys to unlock your potential.*

♋

## YOUR ASCENDED MASTER: ISIS

Queen Goddess Isis encourages a deeper integration of self-care through the ability to manage your own energy and serve from a place of wholeness. As an Ascended Master, she was one of the incarnated deities in Ancient Egypt. She was not only a dedicated wife and mother, but also a powerful spiritual master.

Although she is often primarily associated with her relation to her brother/husband King Osiris and her son, Horus, her family life was tumultuous.[8] After her brother Set kills Osiris, she and her other siblings collect Osiris's body parts because Isis wishes to restore him to life. She utilizes her vast and deep waves of grief—emotions of sorrow, unfulfilled desire, and anger—and magic to perform a soul retrieval[9] (which is, on the material level, an illustration of the mumification process) and sexual ritual to conceive her son, Horus. She cannot bring Osiris back to life, but she restores his soul, so he can live in the afterlife. Known for her compassion and motherly devotion, she protects Horus and eventually assists him in helping him win back the throne from her brother Set.

---

[8] Her mythology is extensive and complex, and there is no way for me to cover it entirely. What I provide here is the basic story and how I interpret it. I encourage you to explore more of the story if you feel drawn to it. There may be other messages and synchronicities within it for you.

[9] A soul retrieval is when we call back the parts of the soul that fled during some sort of trauma. When the soul is deeply wounded, sometimes part of it will leave because it cannot bear the intensity—of emotional and spiritual pain. A soul retrieval can be done through Shamanic practices, magical rituals, hypnosis, or simply during a meditative process.

With her magnificent magical powers and extreme cunning, she eventually avenges the death of her husband and becomes a deity who assists many souls in healing, a guide between the worlds.

The archetype of ♋ exemplifies the mother. Even if you don't have children or you're not a woman, the characteristics of care, affection, devotion, nurturing, and unconditional love are inherent within you.[10] Part of your soul's purpose is to develop these parental traits in your own way, even if only to parent yourself. Therefore, Isis models your potential to embody the mother-like form of feminine strength.

She healed the challenges she faced in her life on Earth through spiritual means. She teaches ♋ that although there may be a situation or person in their life they cannot control, ♋ does have power in their emotions and can, through spiritual healing, balm, soothe, and nurture the soul. When ♋ learns this, they can aid others who seek wholeness and spiritual healing as well.

Isis assists ♋ signs in particular to learn how to give and serve from wholeness. In her story, although she loses her husband, she does not go it alone. She has her siblings to help her, as they heal Osiris in order for him to live in the underworld. Some stories tell about her asking humans

---

[10] Obviously, these traits are still inherent in men and fathers as well, but they are labeled as "motherly" traditionally because they are part of the divine feminine energy that is in all beings. We all have divine masculine energy and divine child energy as well.

♋

to help her on her journey in raising Horus as a now single parent. She understands the need to ask for help from others so she can care for herself, nourishing herself in order to devote so much energy to her loved ones.

Isis encourages you to integrate the wisdom you carry by setting necessary boundaries, taking time to enliven your soul through creativity, and know your priorities.[11] All of these will help you become more balanced and maintain your energy.

One of the reasons why ♋ souls incarnate is to learn to understand the power of their emotions and use them for healing. Goddess Isis assists you to see your significance and have faith that no matter what you do, you are making a difference.

Great Mother Isis greets you:

*Hello, dearest ♋ signs,*
*it is most wise for you*
*to carefully know*
*how your emotions*
*can be helpful,*
*for even though*
*you feel strongly,*
*your heart will show you*
*what is significant.*

---

[11] Doreen Virtue, *Ascended Masters* (Carlsbad, California: Hay House Inc., 2007), 12-3.

*The last and final word
must come, therefore,
not from fear you feel
but rather from what your heart
is whispering to you.*

*Not all emotions are worthwhile.
Wallow only in those that lead you
to where you truly want to go.*

*That is all for now,
but soon you will know more.*

## YOUR RUNE: ANSUZ – ANCESTOR MESSAGES

The Runes, an ancient alphabet and divination tool brought to humanity through Norse God Odin, were and are practiced by Northern European Pagans. Like the Tarot in which each card holds in-depth symbolism and layers of meaning, each Runic glyph carries a well of wisdom. Interpretations of the Runes and even Runic systems vary. (I use the Elder Futhark.)

I have studied formally and formulated personal meanings, but I also receive insights from hearing my ancestors while using the Runes. My ancestor spirit guides speak to me especially clearly through working with the Runes. My heritage includes Danish, Norwegian, Finnish, Cornish and Germanic, all areas where the runes were utilized. These guides lived very closely with the cycles and seasons of the Earth, Sun, Moon, and stars, many of which were farmers and seafarers.

The rune Ansuz literally translates to "a god, ancestral god," and represents the being who is capable of holding and transmitting that energy. In other words, "Ansuz is the receiver-container/transformer-expresser of spiritual power and numinous knowledge," defines Thorsson in *Futhark*.[12] It is my favorite rune, because one of the ways I interpret it is being a channel of divine powers. As a channeler myself, it resonates with the important message of honoring the individual's ability to connect with the spiritual realm. It comes to me through channeling, but

---

[12] Edred Thorsson, *Futhark* (Newburyport, MA: Weiser Books, 2020), 29.

also through intuition and other clair-senses. I believe each of us has the ability to create our own connection with spirit through our extra-sensory abilities.

As a water sign, ♋, you absolutely have the ability to connect with the spiritual realms yourself. It may not be in the same way as I do, but practicing creativity, improving your intuition, bringing through healing powers of the divine through Reiki, or developing your clair-senses is a part of your mission on Earth, so you can bring through Spirit in whatever means you have the inclination to.

For ♋, this rune is also about feeling into your innate power through how you work with your emotions, developing a strong container—that is through creating sacred space and clearing and cleansing your energy regularly—and trusting yourself and your abilities of receiving spiritual messages or energies.

ᚱ

The rune glyph signifies the windblown cloak of Odin, his personification of the Wanderer. As he walked among the mortals, he taught them lessons in hospitality and friendship by posing as a human and sharing stories through poetic verse. So, another interpretation of this rune is inspiration through creative expression. It questions, how can ♋ signs be a parent to others through play and creativity? Sharing the wisdom of the divine, not through authority, but through captivating attention with fun and mystery.

My ancestor guides dance around these core themes by providing insights into how to be a better caretaker and provider, which often starts with how you, ♋, are fully present and provide nourishment to yourself.

My ancestor guides greet you:

*Although dear ♋ signs,*
*you have quite the ability to flow*
*from one thought to another*
*as your emotions carry you there,*
*it is necessary to distinguish*
*between your feelings and those of another,*
*because when you steep all the feelings*
*from other people's souls,*
*you become quite full*
*and are unable to find your center.*

## YOUR NATURE SPIRIT GUIDES: NYMPHS

As the first of the three water signs, ♋ interacts with this element playfully on the surface with ease and flow. The energy of ♋ is not a deep well or murky lake as Scorpio is, nor is ♋ energy a vast endless ocean or sea mist such as Pisces.

Although water can represent many things, most commonly it epitomizes emotions. All the water signs are naturally quite emotional, and it is part of their soul's purpose to learn about emotions and shift them to become beneficial rather than a hinderance.

Therefore, mixing these two concepts, we understand that ♋ signs are here to learn how to float on the emotional surface, not to drown in the depths of despair nor be overwhelmed by the loneliness of open ocean. How can ♋ flow down the stream of ease and trust that the fountain will keep bubbling, that their needs will be met? How can ♋ allow a trickle of emotions to replenish and avoid being a geyser of overreaction?

This is what your nature spirit guides, Nymphs, are here to teach you. They are water elementals who were the mothers and nursemaids of the Greek heroes of mythology. They guard the fertility of Mother Gaia replenishing the soil and maintaining flow and purity in the springs and brooks.[13] When connecting with them, I sense their gentle and graceful energy and feel a stream of calmness flow into me.

---

[13] Teresa Moorey, *The Fairy Bible* (New York: Sterling, 2008), 126.

♋

This type of water elemental reflects your inherent ♋ characteristics, so calling them in will help you in replenishing your sense of self.

Unlike some others, Nymphs are benign nature spirits, but you can always specify this by calling in "benevolent" Nymphs if you wish to connect with them, and if you do sense that you are feeling ungrounded or floaty, all you must do is politely ask them to leave your field of energy.

Feel the soothing encouragement as they greet you:

*A trickle, dear ♋ signs,*
*is just enough sometimes,*
*for even though you wish for more,*
*enough is enough*
*when you allow yourself*
*to release emotions with ease.*

*When you learn to let go slowly and steadily,*
*the painful gush no longer occurs.*
*Once you learn to gaze upon your feelings*
*with ease and recognition,*
*you know that there is no longer*
*a need to feel disdain.*

*Keep trusting that whatever comes up*
*is meant for you to heal,*
*and on the other side of pain*
*will be a beautiful change.*

# MEET YOUR SPIRIT GUIDES

## YOUR ARCHANGEL GUIDE: ARCHANGEL LAVENDER

Archangels, high vibrational beings, sing messages from Source and exude energy of Source. Although referenced in some religious texts, they are not affiliated with any religion. Many of them live a purpose to support humanity, but because humans have free will, we must ask them to help us.

I requested for an Archangel to guide ♋ signs for this book, and Archangel Lavender volunteered! She exemplifies healing through forgiveness and emotional release.

As sensitive water signs, ♋ are very empathetic and receptive to other people's emotions. They have the acute ability to sense what others are feeling. Sometimes, ♋ can even sense when other people are upset with them. They may be able to read when another is holding a grudge or is sending them negative vibes. It can be extremely valuable at times—this 6$^{th}$ sense may be a means of protection or a way to provide care to others in exactly the way they need it—think of it as a heightened parental instinct. However, if ♋ consistently senses strong negative feelings from other people, ♋ may unknowingly create their own grudges, resentments, or attachments, which strengthens unhealthy aspects of any type of relationship.

Archangel Lavender assists ♋ to recognize where they need to forgive another, even if the other person started it. She will assist you in releasing and forgiving hurts from this lifetime and all others. The upsetting emotions you are able to release now will help you forgive yourself and others, no matter how long ago the hurt started. When you take care of your side of the relationship by releasing negative emotions surrounding it, Archangel Lavender will help you clear your Soul Star chakra of the negative energies from other people as well.[14]

Forgiveness is huge, so doing this practice has the potential to be an enormous ascension leap on your soul's journey.

Hear Archangel Lavender's Greeting:

*Hello dear ♋ souls,*
*it is I, Archangel Lavender,*
*here to assist you in healing yourself*
*as well as others.*

*First, I must tell you how necessary it is*
*to take care of yourself first and foremost,*
*for when you care for you,*
*you have the capacity to care for others as well.*
*Only when your cup is full can you treat others*
*with the love that they truly deserve.*

*Next, dear ones, the best method for you*
*is to honor your family by letting go.*
*Listen carefully for this*

---

[14] Diana Cooper, *Archangel Guidebook* (Carlsbad, California: Hay House, 2021), 57.

## MEET YOUR SPIRIT GUIDES

*may not be what you expect to hear.*

*The ancestors you have do not wish you
to repeat the patterns they had.*

*They, even those who seem angry with you
or have disagreements often,
do not fully wish for you
to carry their burdens too.*

*In order to let go of the past,
develop a practice that
releases their negative patterns.*

*I can assist with that.
Allow me to connect to your relatives
to ask their souls to release you.*

*That is all for now, dear ones, more will be
shared in the following sections.*

## YOUR HERB GUIDE: YARROW

Yarrow is a flowering herb of white, yellow, or other pastel colors. Although it can be utilized for many remedies, one of its most valuable characteristics is to help stop bleeding.[15]

All humans have been wounded in one way or another. When we ignore our hurts through denial or by trying to snuff out our emotions, the wound cannot heal and the pain persists, at least on some level. Conversely, but often simultaneously, we identify with a victim mentality. This too keeps the wound from healing.

It is only through acknowledging, feeling, and releasing the pain that the wound will begin to heal.

Bleeding or weeping wounds may manifest as feeling stuck in lower or negative emotions, pitying yourself, or holding on to people or memories that are unhealthy for you.

Even just gazing at the firecracker-like form, light colors, and dainty little flowers Yarrow will put you in a better mood. The pungent yet sweet top-note aroma transports you to a new level. Yarrow reminds you to take the baby steps and subtle shifts to transition into the healed version of you.

---

[15] Josie, *Materia Medica* (St. Paul, MN: Tenderheart Studio, 2021), 25.

# MEET YOUR SPIRIT GUIDES

Yarrow uses tough love, joy, and delight to help you stop bleeding.

Herb Yarrow says hello:

*Yellow!*
*Dear ♋ signs,*
*that is, hello to you,*
*for when you brighten up your mood*
*you will enjoy some puns too.*

*It's nearly upon you,*
*the ability to let go of those emotions*
*that have been long stuck in your soul.*

*It is necessary, then, to see*
*how the bold and bright yellow of the Sun*
*can cause you to be a bit more cheery.*

*We know you like the moonlit shadows of night*
*and enjoy the salty sulkiness of the sea,*
*but come out of the depth and see*
*how bright and beautiful the world can be.*

*We know you have been*
*working on letting go*
*for quite some time,*
*but all you have to do*
*is gradually change your focus*

♋

*and remember you are truly, wholly alive!*

*Rejoice in it!*

MEET YOUR SPIRIT GUIDES

## YOUR TAROT GUIDE: PAGE OF PENTACLES

Pages have a child-like enthusiasm, seeing the world with a sense of wonder. They explore, fascinate, and do not worry about falling down, for they will just get up again as if nothing ever happened.

As a ruler of the pentacles suit, they are out in the world experiencing what it is like to be material and to live tangibly with excitability, delighting in the sensory facets of life.

♋ signs are often likened to mothers because they have an innate nurturing, nourishing and caring quality to them. Regardless of whether they are male or female, how old they are, and if they ever have children, they carry parental characteristics.

For ♋ signs, Page-of-Pentacle-type people are important for them. ♋ feels useful when they are expressing their love by caring and guiding others. Yes, often ♋ signs get to nourish Page of Pentacle people in a parental-like way, but just as importantly these Pages teach ♋ signs how to let go and enjoy the present, how to bring back their sense of wonderment, and how to live a life of naïve excitement.

So, what Page-of-Pentacle-type people can you invite into your life? For some ♋ signs they may literally be children, for others they may be students or clients, for some they may be a friend or family member who never lost their childlike wonder (perhaps a youthful Earth sign, like a fairy-loving Taurus).

♋

It is important to remember that as the parental-like figure in this relationship you will be guiding, nurturing, or caring for the other in one way or another, but they are also there to teach you. Ponder what they are demonstrating with their child-like wisdom of the world.

Hear this initial message from Page of Pentacles:

*You are wise, dear ♋ signs,*
*to grab a steady hold of your footing,*
*for you don't want to be*
*swept away by the waves.*

*I am here, dear ♋ crabs to tell you*
*how to laugh, how to enjoy,*
*and how to determine decisively*
*what it is your heart wants to manifest.*

*For in your watery ways,*
*you may ebb one way and then another,*
*not sure of how to decide.*
*You easily pick up stories of others*
*and believe them to be your own.*

*It is time to create your own life now.*
*Not the one that has been*
*modeled to you someway, somehow.*
*Sure, take bits and pieces of ideas,*

*but ground your truth of pursuit
that truly fits your interests.*

*That is all for now,
more to be explored later.
Toodaloo!*

♋

## YOUR TREE: OAK

What sets Oak apart from other trees? Perhaps his sturdiness, his posture, his ancient wisdom canopying several centuries, or his lobey-leaves. Yes, but I would say his ability to stand on his own.

Most trees thrive especially heartily in a forest, giving and receiving nutrients through the roots and fungi networks underneath the ground. Oaks do fine in a forest. But unlike others, they likewise shine when they stand alone. Imagine the quintessential Oak not only standing tall, straight, and strong, but also expanding with a massive trunk and sprawling branches in the middle of a rolling countryside or in a lucky person's backyard.

Because of his sturdiness and strong, durable wood, Oak is associated with masculine energy. Zeus as the mighty patriarch protecting gods and humans alike claims Oak as his sacred tree, and in the northern tradition, Oak is (somewhat conversely knowing Zeus's libertine mythology) associated with a strong, steadfast, and supportive husband, someone you can lean on.

In this regard, Oak proves to be a guide to help ♋ balance their energy. Often ♋ can be overly supple like a Weeping Willow, and Oak teaches ♋ to find people in their life who are like Oak: a faithful partner, a loyal friend, a strong advisor, a wise elder, people ♋ can rely on regardless of what part of the cycle they are in or what mood they are embodying.

But Oak also teaches ♋ how to build their own strength and stand up for themselves.

When ♋ signs rely too much on others or become too pliable to other people's needs, they will benefit from modeling Oak's example to stand alone, growing and expanding through their sole strength. When ♋ learns how to do this, they can thrive in all conditions; they are hearty whether they live alone or are surrounded by others.

Listen to Oak's first message to you:

*Hello, dear ♋ friends,*
*your world is being turned upside down*
*if you are unable*
*to let your roots grow more.*

*This is important for you*
*because without stable footing,*
*you cannot move forward.*

*What is most necessary for you to do,*
*is to create a structure of support around you.*

*How do you do that, Oak, you ask?*
*Well, I am here to tell you that.*

*The easiest way for you to do so*
*is to reach out to others.*

♋

*Nourish them with your care,
and you will find them supporting you.*

*Just as roots reach out and form structure,
these bonds are not publicly seen,
but rather are alliances formed
underneath the surface:*

*Ones that are not seeking recognition
but rather are private—
your nearest and dearest ones will give you
the structure and support to grow.*

## YOUR RULING PLANET: THE MOON

The Moon inspires us with a sense of wonderment. Her enduring changes are visible as she ebbs and flows, waning into a sliver and waxing into a glowing sphere. Sometimes completely invisible and other times peeking through the daytime atmosphere, surprising us with delight when she still manages to glow in the bright light of the day. As she revolves around us, she is the quickest moving Celestial Being, traversing through the signs for only a few days at a time.

As our Celestial Mother, she provides us with rhythm, reminding us: we don't always have to be "on," it is okay to take a break, we need to rest, we are loved no matter what.

Because she is your ruler (♋ being the first of the water signs) and she causes the tides of our waters, she is known for her emotional pull. Connecting with her means tuning into your emotions, following your whims, and nourishing your Spirit. In *The Book of the Moon*, Steven Forrest reminds us that the Moon is also our secret to happiness by briefly slipping out of the world of reason, proficiency, ought to, and responsibility, all of the things that slightly suppress the inclinations of the soul.[16] In other words, the Moon gives you permission to follow your fancy and forget about obligations for a while.

---

[16] Steven Forrest, *The Book of the Moon* (Borrego Springs, CA: Seven Paws Press, 2010), 18.

♋

🌙

She personifies the flowing feminine energy, and the astrological glyph that represents her shows only one of her many phase-points. Her characteristics can be used as a model for *anyone* who wants to tap into the cycles of life-death-rebirth.

She reminds us that it is healthy to let go, and in doing so, we are able to allow in new things. For ♋ signs in particular, it is important to use the waning energy of the moon to release the past. Doing so will make ♋ feel so much better. Because ♋ is a water sign, releasing involves more than just letting go of the material, but also releasing the emotional baggage and the spiritual connections to past people, places, and situations. Emotionally, using practices such as EFT tapping or Qi Gong shaking would be extremely helpful. Spiritually, cutting cords, attachments, and enmeshments is essential.

I cannot emphasize enough the importance of the cycle when speaking of the Moon. Not only the waxing into full moon and waning into new moon, but also her movement through the signs. This comes through when I channel her. During an Aries waxing crescent phase, she will be bolder and more insistent. While she is in a Libra waxing gibbous phase, she is pleasant and maturely helpful. I decided to channel all of the material for this book during her waning crescent ♋ phase, as it felt like what was most needed for this book. Because of this, her messages are fairly brief and profoundly honest, no sugar-coating during the balsamic phase in ♋.

The Moon greets you:

> *Listen carefully dear ones,*
> *Your time is reaching*
> *a new cycle and with it*
> *comes turmoil.*
>
> *As you see,*
> *nearly all you were once*
> *under the tides of pain*
> *in one way or another,*
> *and your vast understanding*
> *is Waxing.*
>
> *For during your deepest*
> *emotional unrest*
> *comes a seed of newness,*
> *so do not be alarmed,*
> *for all is as it should be.*
> *The next step for you*
> *is glowing more and more,*
> *and when the cycle ends,*
> *a new one begins.*
>
> *The most important thing*
> *to remember*

♋

*is to not get pulled under
but rather,
float with the flowing emotions knowing
that there will be a breakthrough.*

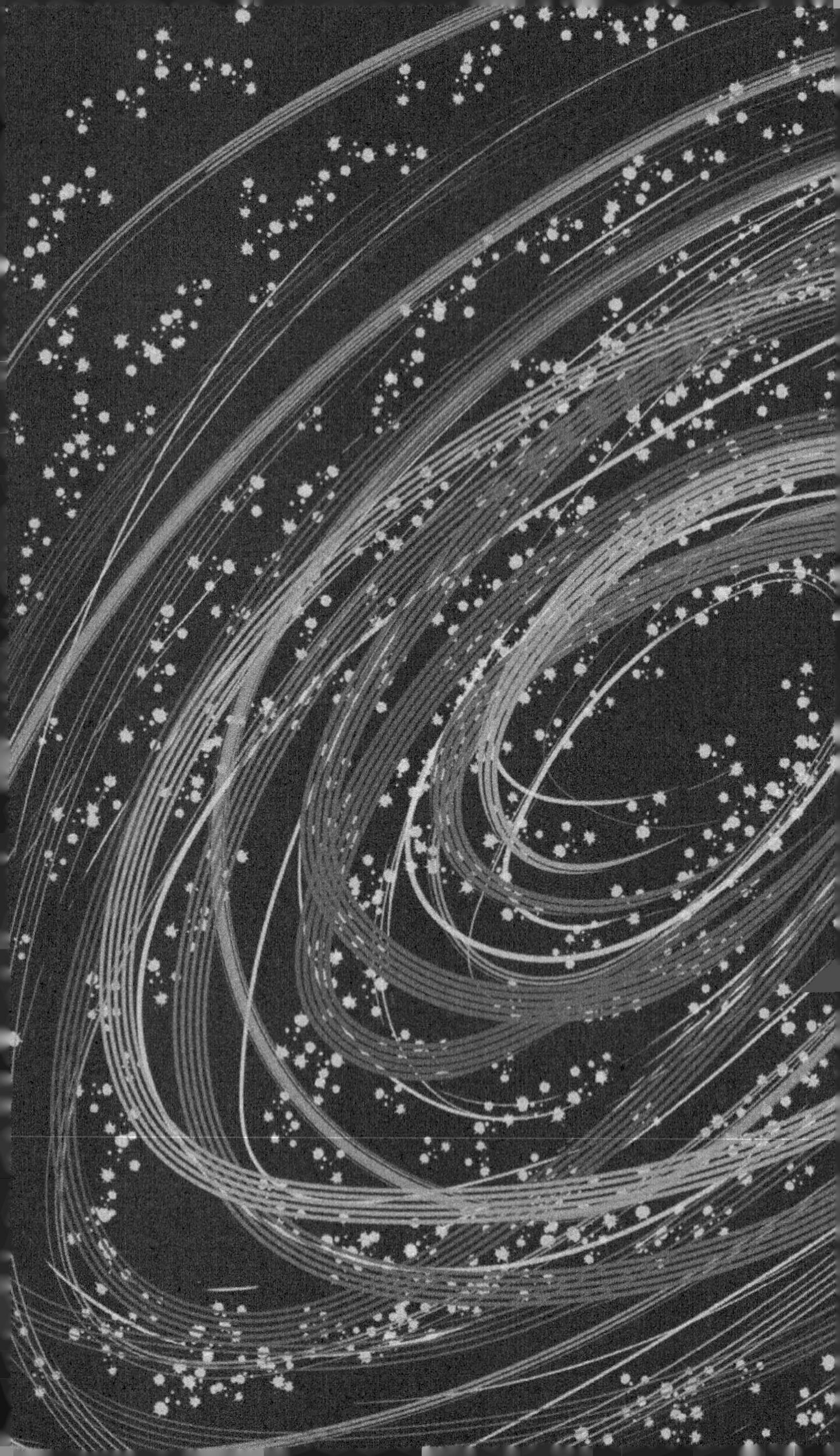

# HOW CAN ♋ NURTURE SUCCESS IN WORK AND BUSINESS?

## CRAB

*While we do wish for you,
dear ♋ signs,
to find success in work and business,*

*it may not be what you think,
for you define your own
sense of success.*

*Rather than managing or
filing or promoting,
you may be interested
in serving or helping.*

*Rather them hauling in
heaps of treasure,
your biggest success may
be nourishing others.*

*When you shed the plan
you thought would bring you gold,
you realize the fulfillment comes
from a sideways path.*

WORK | BUSINESS

## **LAPIS LAZULI**

*Listen dear ♋ signs,*
*your work is best for you*
*when you care about what you do.*

*How can you either find a way*
*to care for what you already do*
*or move to a new career*
*that you truly care for?*

*This is what you can ask,*
*then wait and see*
*what will manifest.*

♋

## ISIS

*Hello dearest ♋ signs,*
*although your heart is in your home,*
*your work and business are also significant.*

*Rewire your thinking to see*
*how your business is not you,*
*and you are not your family.*

*When you allow yourself some separation,*
*you come to realize that*
*even though you love both,*
*the attention you need is on yourself.*

*Once you spend more time caring for you*
*and you take into account all the things you do*
*that give you nourishment to serve*
*from a place of security,*
*your work will be easy.*

*It does not matter how long it takes to heal,*
*for when you are feeling fully nourished,*
*your business and work will still be there.*

WORK | BUSINESS

## ANSUZ - ANNA'S ANCESTOR GUIDES

*We want to tell you, dearies,
that work is not what it used to be.*

*For back long ago, it was
tending to the body and community.*

*This is perhaps where you resonate still,
so discover how to make it your lifelong goal.*

♋

## NYMPHS

*One, two, three . . .
You see, dear ♋ signs,
that sometimes you have to try
before things begin to flow.*

*It is not that they aren't meant to be,
but rather that a lesson needed to be learned.*

*So, keep up the good work,
and when you are ready for more,
then you will be capable of more.*

## ARCHANGEL LAVENDER

*Listen, dear ♋ souls,*
*it is I, Archangel Lavender,*
*here to assist you in knowing more*
*about your soul's work.*

*You see, dear ones, the work you do*
*is not all for money in a firm or business,*
*but rather for your soul.*

*In many ways the most important work you can do*
*may not even be known by anyone but you.*

*That is doing the work to heal your soul*
*and the energies of those connected to you.*

*When you look into the past*
*and see what needs recognized,*
*it can be healed with compassionate eyes.*

*Energize yourself by loving*
*yourself on all levels*
*and welcoming in what it means to feel whole,*
*those parts of you that were not held before.*

*When you care for*
*these parts of your soul,*

♋

*your nourishing energy grows,
and you are capable to better serve others
regardless of if you work in a firm or at home.*

WORK | BUSINESS

## YARROW

*Yikes, dear ♋ signs,
have you been sweeping
something under the rug?*

*You see, it is most important,
yes, to follow your whims
and flow with the tides
but you must also learn to
get out of the sand
and be diligent with your plans.*

*Take time to cultivate a more rigid structure
at times when you feel washed away
and out of control, for you are
much stronger than you realize.*

*Take note of how long
it is necessary for you to rest
and take care
because these are important for you.*

*But get out of bed and get to work
when you are called to.*

♋

## PAGE OF PENTACLES

*Have you, dear ♋ signs,
been listening to
too much advice on
how others make it work?*

*It is now time to let go
of all those ideas
and come up with your own
now that you are informed.*

*How can you make your day
filled with happiness and bliss?*

*What will lighten your load?
It is not necessary
to reinvent the wheel,
but when you follow too closely
what others are already doing,
you miss the chance to step into
your own unique mission.*

*Take time today to figure it out,
ask your intuition what is truly best for you,
and you may be surprised
that your target was
not what you expected.*

WORK | BUSINESS

## OAK

*First, dear ♋ friends,*
*hear me out,*
*you must learn how to use*
*your sensitivity to your advantage.*

*Although not all workplaces*
*are conducive to your empathy,*
*if you are intentional*
*about your alliances*
*and sensitive to others needs,*
*you will find that in just the right time,*
*whatever you have been wanting to do*
*will come to you with ease.*

*Use your intuition to find out*
*who to connect with and*
*who to go without.*

♋

## MOON

*Dear ♋ signs, it is I, your Moon,*
*who wishes you to see*
*how not everything*
*must be done at once.*

*For when you*
*follow the rhythm*
*of growth and decay,*
*you will know*
*that the harvest will be great.*

*But when you expect*
*the seeds to sprout*
*before they are ready,*
*they will not produce with plenty.*

WORK | BUSINESS

## MOST TREASURED TAKEAWAYS

- If you define your own success, you may realize it is easier for you to grasp than you had originally imagined.
- It is so important for you to care about the work you do, so either make adjustments to enjoy your work where you are now or set the intention to do something new.
- Instead of pouring all your energy into your family and work, take some time for yourself. If you do so, you will be fully ready to have a thriving business.
- Tending to your body and your community may be your calling as it was for people long ago.
- Just because things are not working out for you doesn't mean they aren't meant to be. It may be that you must continue through to learn a lesson that you need to before things flow easier.
- The most important work you can do is soul work. Welcome back parts of you that need healing still. When you nourish these parts of you, you will be able to better serve others.
- Although you love living in flow, consider adding more structure to your work, for this will allow your strength to shine through. You are stronger than you think.
- ♋ signs may not necessarily be great at business (depending on their other chart placements), so they often seek other's advice.

But there comes a point when they need to stop copying and tune into their own unique soul's mission.
- Use your sensitivity to your advantage by connecting to your intuition to allow it to tell you who your best work alliances will be.
- Follow the pattern the Moon models to you. When you learn that there is a time for growth and a time for decay, your business will thrive.

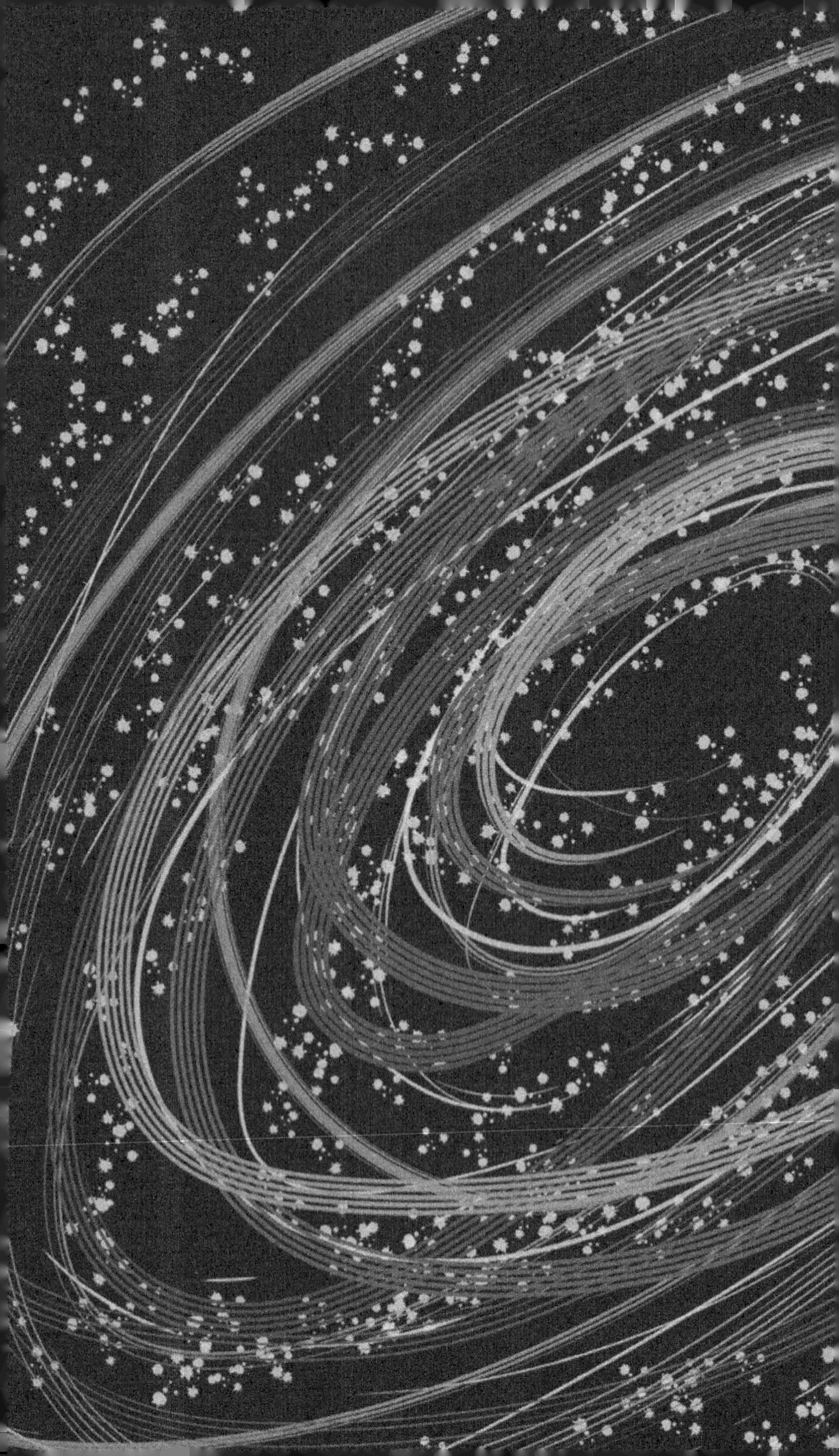

# HOW CAN ♋ NURTURE WEALTH AND ABUNDANCE?

♋

## CRAB

*Under your shell, dear ♋ signs,
you are quite supple,
so take note of how this can
be worthwhile.*

*For instance, you need to build
a shell, a structure, or a container
to fill your cup, and then you will
have the resources within
to give and serve
however you see fit.*

*Only when your cup is full
do you have the energy to give.
So, find your source of nourishment,
give the overflow to others
and watch it rain.*[17]

---

[17] I believe this is a play on the idiom "make it rain," meaning bring in prosperity through work. In this case you are watching it rain by allowing prosperity to flow to you. A subtle, yet important difference.

ABUNDANCE

## LAPIS LAZULI

*Even though you often
wear your heart on your sleeve,
you sometimes forget how easily
you give up on your dreams,
for there is always someone else
to care for and nurture,
always someone else in need.*

*But know that the more wealth you cultivate,
the more resources you will have to give
from a place of abundance.*

♋

## ISIS

*Did you know, dearest ♋ signs,
in the midst of caring for yourself,
you let your true value shine?*

*When you take care of you
from a place of self-love,
this attention illustrates how valued
you see yourself as.*

*So even though it seems counterproductive,
the time you spend on pampering yourself
leads you to even greater wealth.*

## ANSUZ – ANNA'S ANCESTOR GUIDES

*Did you know, dearies,
when you sow the seeds
in the evening, they have time
to germinate in the darkness,
and once the sunlight shines again,
they will be ready
to push forth out of the dirt?*

*This is what you must do,
many of you, must first go within
and find out how to germinate,
then when you are ready to grow,
the sun will shine upon you.*

♋

## NYMPHS

*Did you know, dear ♋ signs,*
*that water flows downstream?*
*This is easy for you to see*
*but let us express the concept.*

*The best brooks are the ones*
*that have plenty moving quickly*
*for stagnancy is never a nicety.*

*But when you don't have much,*
*the flow can slow, and you can't let go.*

*When you have plenty,*
*that is when things move quickly.*
*So, although you are nervous to spend more*
*when you have little,*
*know that when you make more*
*the flow out will be comfortable.*

*So rather than cutting expenses,*
*learn how to bring more in,*
*and in doing so, you will*
*also have more to give.*

## ABUNDANCE

## ARCHANGEL LAVENDER

*Hello dear ♋ souls,
it is I, Archangel Lavender,
here to assist you with bringing in abundance,
or rather, seeing how abundant you are.*

*The most important thing for you to know
is that you are capable.
You have the ability to make or create
whatever you need to live comfortably.*

*But wherever you doubt your own abilities,
you shut it out.*

*So rather than conspiring
on how it is you will make more,
think of how you have done so much already,
how wonderful you are,
and how much nourishment
you have to give.*

*Once you recognize
your capacity to create wealth
is far bigger
than you thought before
and allow in more,
you will see abundance flow.*

## YARROW

*Where is your focus,
dear ♋ signs?*

*Is it on lack
or is it on abundance?*

*Take note of all the good you have
surrounding you and blessing you,
for you do have wonderful things
to be very grateful for.*

*When you look at all those blessings
instead of what you lack,
your mind turns upside-down,
and in comes your flow of cash.*

## PAGE OF PENTACLES

*We know, dear ♋ signs,*
*that many of you like best*
*to put your head in the sand*
*in regard to coming up with*
*a financial plan.*

*But, as you see, it is quite necessary*
*for you to understand*
*with some sense of clarity*
*how to make your money work.*

*If you need a helping hand,*
*ask someone to assist you*
*and do not be frightened*
*when they tell you the value,*
*for you can flow easier than most*
*so allow the knowledge*
*to set you in the right direction.*

♋

## OAK

*Do you see, dear ♋ friends,
that the structure you have
needs an adjustment?*

*Look at where your finances are going
and see how to align them more
with the things you value most.*

*If something does not fulfill your needs,
cancel the payment.*

*Once you determine how
to allocate with more awareness,
you will see how
the money that you save
can become a bigger asset.*

## ABUNDANCE

## MOON

*Careful dear ♋ signs,*
*for wealth may be elusive.*

*When you focus your attention*
*upon money, you may see it*
*as a slippery slope,*
*illusionary.*

*Instead, learn to regard your wealth*
*as the fullness of your health,*
*as the vastness of your ancestral support,*
*and as the abundance of your worth!*

## MOST TREASURED TAKEAWAYS

- If you build your own reserve first, then you will *effortlessly* be able to share with others. With a wealth of energy, you will easily give. Then just watch the abundance flow in.
- There is always going to be someone needing your attention, and you may have been putting your dreams aside because of them. But you'll be able to serve more when you grow your resources from following your passion.
- When you show yourself that you are valuable by giving yourself what you need, others will see your value too and your wealth will grow.
- Wealth takes time to grow. Plant the seeds and wait while you prepare, and when you are ready, the sun will shine on you.
- Instead of cutting your expenses, learn how you can earn more. This will make the flow more sustainable.
- When you focus on how capable you are, how much you have already done, and all the amazing things you offer to others, you will see abundance flow.
- Examine where you are putting your attention. Is it on lack or on abundance? Focus on your blessings and watch good things come to you.
- Gaining clarity on your finances will set you in the right direction, even through it may be uncomfortable in the beginning.

## ABUNDANCE

- Do you still align with all of the subscriptions and services you are paying for? If not, make the adjustment needed and your savings will be worthwhile.
- Abundance is so much more than money. See wealth in your health, your ancestral support, and your self-worth.

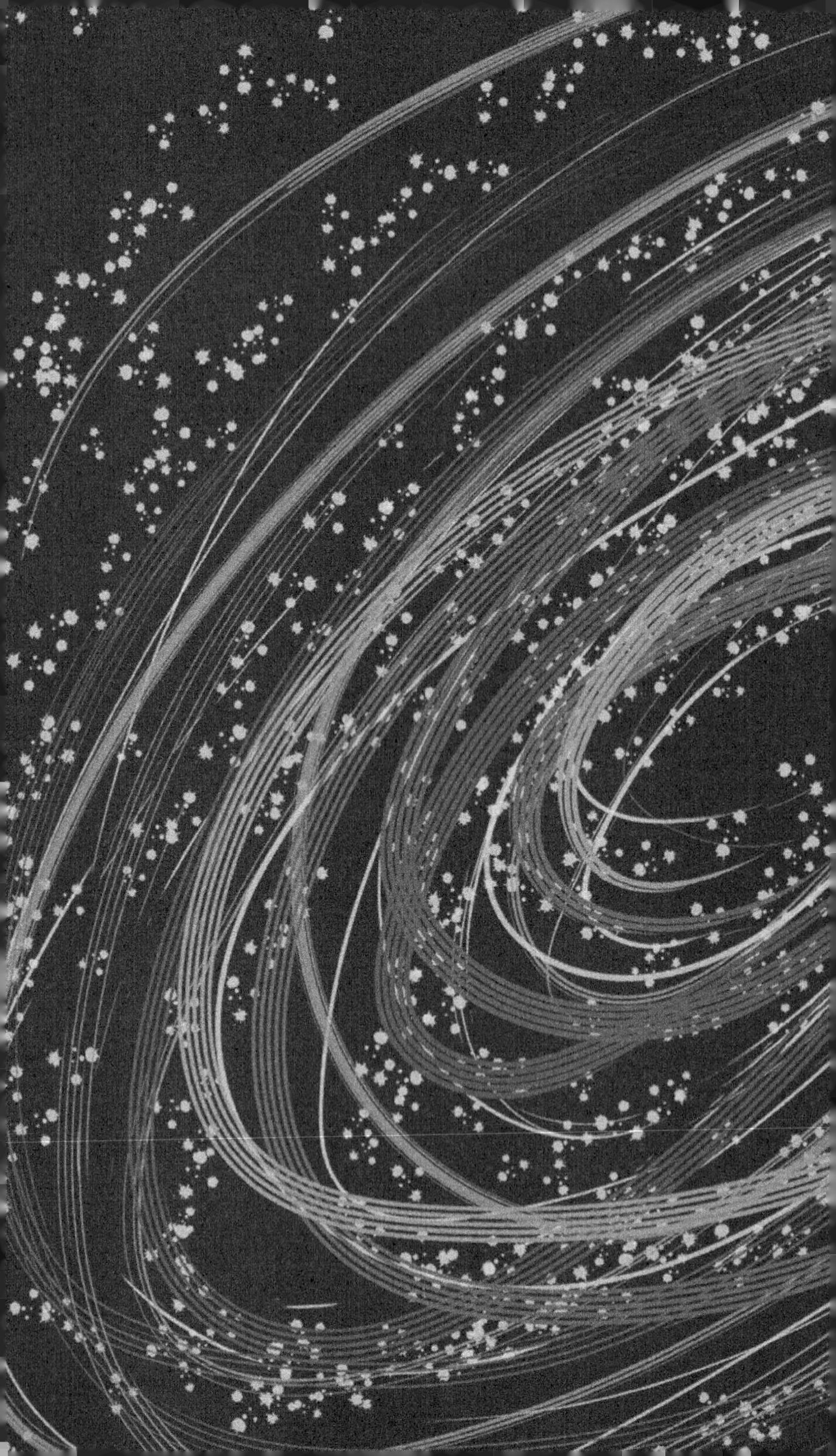

# HOW CAN ♋ NURTURE SUCCESS IN LOVE?

♋

## CRAB

*We have a story for you, dear ♋ signs,*
*and it goes along the lines*
*of truth about your existence.*

*Once upon a time, there was*
*a bucket full of crabs.*
*How they all got in there*
*is not that important,*
*because we all find ourselves in*
*a rut once in a while*
*and so do you, dear ♋ signs.*

*In this bucket there were many crabs,*
*and they all loved one another quite readily,*
*for one would stand on another's back*
*to receive help and vice versa.*

*They were all quite crowded,*
*and one crab, in particular,*
*was wondering what*
*could possibly be beyond*
*the life in a pail.*

*She found a way to crawl*
*and scrape up the side*
*enough to reach the lip of the bucket.*

## LOVE

*She clamped her pincher tightly
and was determined to pull herself up.
But once the other crabs saw her,
they began to grab ahold of her.
Rather than needing to only
pull the weight of her own shell,
she realized she had a dozen
others to pull up as well.*

*At first, she tried with all her might
to give it a go,
but realized soon
that it was impossible.
She let go.*

*This, dear ♋, seems like quite a sad tale,
yet it is not quite over.*

*She pondered for several days
about what she must do
to get out of the bucket
and onto the sand,
for she knew she needed water instinctively
and also longed to have a space of her own.*

*After having posed the question,
her mind began to race at an astounding pace.
The ideas poured in like a waterfall,*

♋

*and soon she received one
that she managed to catch with her claw.
This idea was to see
if the crabs
would work together
to all get out
of the bucket forever.*

*Rather than each trying to climb one at a time,
they would all lean against one side
and perhaps the bucket would tip.*

*She tried to explain to the other crabs
the goal of this pursuit
but none of them understood
what she was talking about.
Rather than trying to explain again,
she just instructed them how to stand
and where and when to heave,
and although they did not get it fully,
they agreed to try it out.*

*Sure enough, with the might of many,
the crabs tipped the bucket,
and they were all set free.*

*The moral of the story is to flip your plan.
Instead of using all your might*

## LOVE

*to help everyone else,*
*give them the instructive tools*
*to teach them how to help themselves,*
*and you will be set free in the process.*

♋

## LAPIS LAZULI

*Careful, dear ♋ signs,*
*for your heart is rather tender,*
*and although you wish*
*it not to be so sometimes,*
*it is not up to you,*
*for its part of your true nature.*

*So rather than fighting yourself*
*on how sensitive you are,*
*realize that with your tender heart,*
*you have the capacity to love*
*even more than others,*
*for when you let your emotions flow freely,*
*you see that the rains bring in roses.*

## ISIS

*There is a story I wish to share with you,
dearest ♋ signs,
It is not all so easy to hear,
but will provide you
with a knowing deep inside,
that will give you exactly what you need.*

*There was once a little bee, a Bumble Bee,
who wished very much to be seen,
for she had lost her ability to shine brightly.
She had instead been busy
assisting those around her.*

*You may know, dearest ♋ signs,
that this story is about more than just a bee
but rather is a way for me to tell you of your life.*

*This little bee, her name is Ginny,
and she was always so focused
on how to serve the hive,
what could she do to help all the others?
For they needed her, at least
this is what she thought.*

*Little Ginny was buzzing around one day
when she realized that she had been annoyed.*

♋

*Poor me, she thought, for her energy was low,*
*and no one seemed to recognize all the effort*
*she was putting in to care for them.*

*Alas, another bee from the colony,*
*who happened to be Ginny's friend,*
*got so upset that day*
*she stung a passerby*
*who had tried to swat at her like a fly.*

*As you may know, dearest ♋ signs,*
*when a Bumble Bee stings, it also dies.*

*Ginny was so distraught by this calamity*
*that she nearly stung herself to death in the process.*

*How had she not known*
*her friend needed assistance?*
*How did she not see the signs?*

*She had been so focused upon everyone else*
*all the time, that the dearest to her*
*did not receive the attention they deserved.*

*But once Ginny calmed down after the tragedy,*
*she realized that nothing she would have done*
*could have saved her dear friend,*
*for how could she control another's reaction?*

## LOVE

*It is not possible.*

*But although this story
has a tragic element to it,
it is not all bad.*

*For Ginny, upon seeing this hurt
decided that no matter what,
she would take care of herself
first and foremost.*

*For the love she gave herself,
although it had been little then,
in comparison to how it was now,
had saved her from overreacting
to something she had no power over.*

*She saw how her life was blessed
by this message she had received,
for even though her friend had died,
her Bumble soul had flown away
into a better place.*

## ANSUZ – ANNA'S ANCESTOR GUIDES

*This topic, dearies, is close to our hearts,
for in love you find reason to live
upon this beautiful Earth.*

*We find it troubling that although
many of you are quite loving,
you forget sometimes that you
first must love yourself first,
and once you figure that out,
you will know how to love another fully
without clinging to their soul.*

*Find your strength through love,
and you will see how easy it is to love deeply,
yet unconditionally.*

LOVE

## NYMPHS

*We love you, dear ♋ signs,*
*for even though*
*you are temperamental,*
*you have lots to give.*

*Your love is like a waterfall,*
*listen carefully as to why this is.*

*Love is never-ending and flows from up above.*
*It comes from a source that is not seen,*
*and it makes its way with ease.*
*Once at the bottom, it pools*
*and can be stored if it has the capacity.*

*So, think of your love in this way,*
*and you will never run out.*

♋

## ARCHANGEL LAVENDER

*Oh listen carefully, dear ♋ souls,
for this is as important as ever now.
It is I, Archangel Lavender,
here to assist you on creating
more love in your life.*

*Firstly, dear ones, even the littlest rendition
of love is important;
no matter how small the gesture,
it is worthwhile.*

*So, when you give a kiss to one you love,
or when you give someone a hug,
or when you write a note
showing your affection,
these little gestures end up being very large.*

*For when another is having a bad day,
or at least they perceive it that way,
and you come in and brighten their day,
even if it doesn't seem significant to you,
it could make the difference in their life
between feeling alone and unworthy
to feeling loved and valued.*

*So continue spreading your love in small ways,*

# LOVE

*for they add up to something big
in the grand scheme of things.*

♋

## YARROW

*Oh, dear ♋ signs,*
*your heart is overflowing*
*with love at times,*
*but it may also overflow*
*with hate if you do not learn to let go*
*of those emotions that are causing rot.*

*Keep listening*
*even though it is hard to hear.*

*Is there someone*
*or something that happened*
*that you are clinging to?*
*Is there a hardness somewhere*
*inside of you?*

*When you allow that hate to dissipate,*
*you open up your heart to a new start,*
*and no matter if you are alone*
*or with another already,*
*your fresh start*
*will allow you*
*to fully feel love again.*

LOVE

## PAGE OF PENTACLES

*What does your heart say, dear ♋ signs?*

*For your emotions will ebb and flow,
changing as quickly as the tide,
but the steady beat of your heart
will be more consistent than that.*

*So quiet down and see
who or what
your heart is whispering about.*

## OAK

*One love, dear ♋ friends,
does not stand before another.*

*Listen carefully,
the world is full of many people
who are important to you,
because your heart has warmth
beyond what others often do.*

*Because of this,
your love may feel differently.
When you see that
no one is needing all your love,
but rather, you can spread it out with ease.*

*Just because you feel love for many,
does not mean you do not care fully.*

LOVE

## MOON

*Dear ♋ signs,
your heart may be tender
to all others
but the most sensitive significance
should be on yourself.*

*Hear me now.*

*The care and attention
you place on yourself
is what creates security,
for even though your
love is widely known and felt,
you must learn to plant it as a tree.*

*The roots will feed you
from the land and sea.
The steady trunk is you
standing strongly centered in self
as the branches are your open arms.*

*Make sure to nourish yourself before all else.*

## MOST TREASURED TAKEAWAYS

- When you teach others how to help themselves, you have less of a burden for yourself.
- Your sensitivity is a part of you. When you allow your tears to flow, you let in more love.
- It is impossible to control another's reactions and decisions. So, although you can do the best you can to take care of another, the best thing for you to do is to take care of yourself before all others.
- When you figure out how to love yourself first, you develop a deep unconditional connection with others.
- Think of how love is like an always-flowing waterfall, and you will always feel full of love.
- Even the littlest gestures of love can become really significant for the one who is receiving them.
- When you allow any and all hate to be released, your heart will heal, and you will be able to truly begin again.
- It may not be reliable to listen to your emotions, for they ebb and flow. But when you tune in to your heart, you will know, with surety, your direction.
- You may feel equally loving and caring to many who you love. Do not think this in any way diminishes it.
- Your foundation comes from receiving nourishment from the land and sea, structure

## LOVE

and flow, and when you're centered in self, you
can expand your arms to nourish others as well.

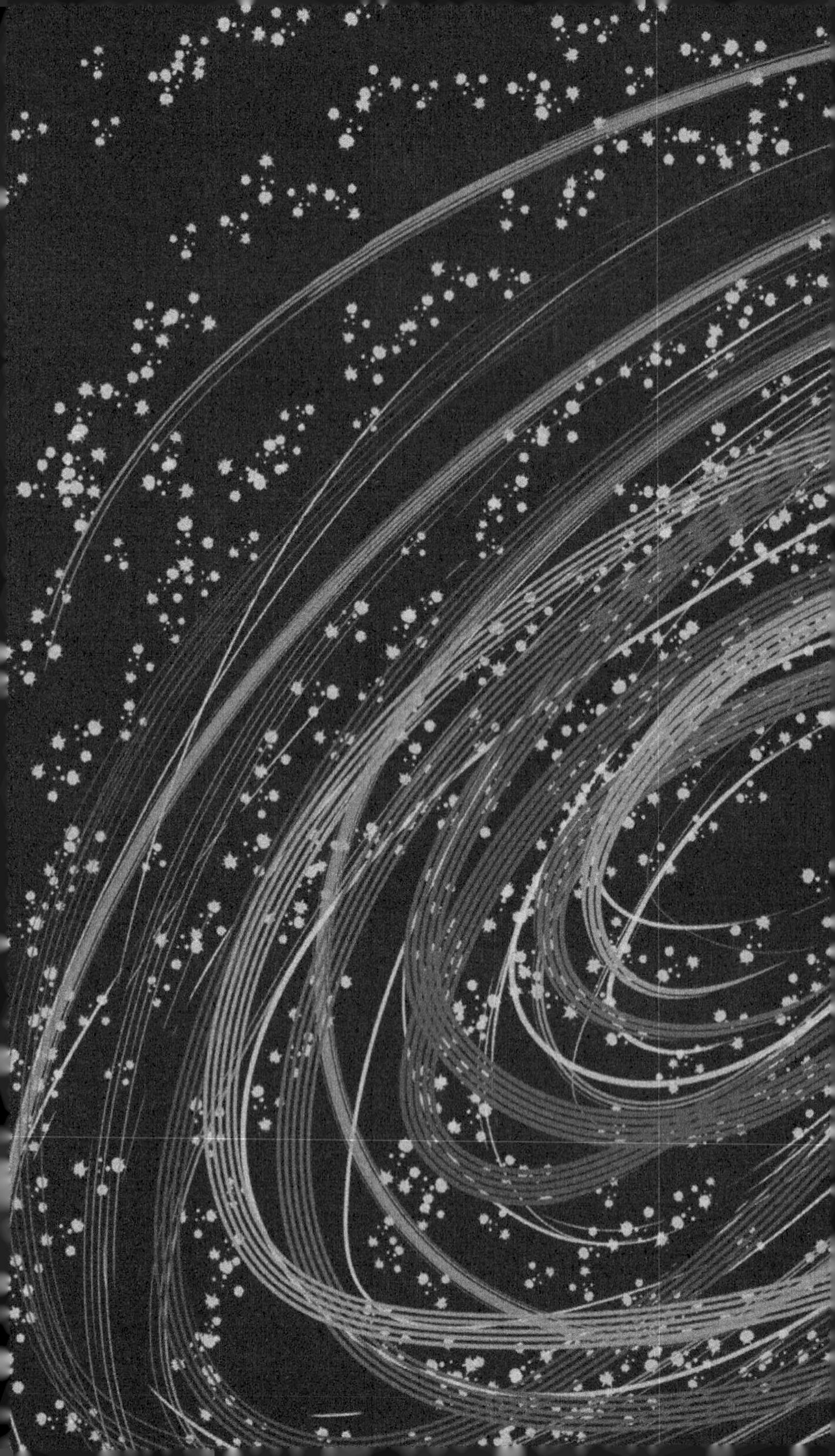

# HOW CAN ♋ NURTURE MEANINGFUL RELATIONSHIPS?

♋

## CRAB

*You, dear ♋, have much to learn still,
for even though your close friends
and family are dear to your heart,
you must allow them more freedom.*

*You see, there is a tendency
to cling to nostalgic times,
and sometimes it is best
to see how allowing others to grow
can also set you free.*

*Now, you may be wondering
what this means,
for not all of you
are physically attached,
but the thoughts you think
about another
create a cord,
and the longing you feel
creates entanglement.*

*You must use the power of your pinchers
to cut these attachments
in order to live with more sense
of your own assurance.*

## LAPIS LAZULI

*It feels necessary for you,
dear ♋ signs, to care for your family
above all else, whether they be close or far,
for your ties to them established who you are now.*

*Rather than holding tight
to the memories that you once had of them,
allow them to grow and expand,
for that is the kindest most caring gift
you can offer them.*

♋

## ISIS

*You know, dearest ♋ signs,
the ones that are dear to you
are never alone.*

*This is important for you to know,
because, hear me out,
you are not the only one
for them to rely on.*

*Although it is so wonderful, ♋ signs,
that you care and nourish those you love,
they have others to assist them too.
Do not take it all upon yourself.*

*Now some may not believe this to be so,
but even those who seem to be alone
have assistance from Spirit.*

*So, if you ever have a friend
or family member in need,
instead of over-extending,
send an angel to assist them.*

FRIENDS | FAMILY

## ANSUZ - ANNA'S ANCESTOR GUIDES

*Although we may not come from
the same tribe, dear ♋ signs,
that does not mean we are enemies.*

*Think of how close to your heart
you call your dearest friends and family.
Now imagine how the whole world
is one big family.*

*The reason you cling so tightly
to those you hold dear,
is because on a certain level
you fear being alone.*

*But no matter what you feel,
come to understand
that all humans are one clan,
and when we stick together,
regardless of our names, titles, or race,
we will become one, and
hate will be erased.*

## NYMPHS

*Shower those you love and care for,*
*dear ♋ signs,*
*with love and nourishment.*

*When you give blessings to them with purity,*
*they will feel the difference.*

*Rather than giving them care*
*from a place of obligation,*
*give them nurturing*
*from your heart center.*
*The way you must do this*
*is to fill your cup first.*

FRIENDS | FAMILY

## ARCHANGEL LAVENDER

*Hello dear ♋ souls,*
*it is I, Archangel Lavender,*
*here to assist you on developing relationships.*

*When your home is filled with people you love,*
*it makes you feel at home.*

*Even though these ones you care for*
*can be difficult at times,*
*their presence fills your heart with joy.*

*When, dear ones, it becomes too much,*
*you may realize that it is time*
*to take a deferment*
*and care for those connections*
*by clearing and cleansing them.*

*When you wish to have an easier time*
*caring for the ones you love,*
*make sure your connection is bathed in love*
*and that you nurture yourself*
*by refreshing the energy*
*between you and your loved ones.*

♋

## YARROW

*Keep in mind, dear ♋ signs,
that when you are away,
it is the best time to find yourself.*

*Let me explain.*

*Sometimes you have a tendency,
dear ♋ signs, to meld with others
and do what they say
rather than acknowledging what you feel.*

*You are quite sensitive,
and although this is a strong suit,
if you are not first secure with yourself,
you cannot know where you end
and another begins.*

*So go away from friends and family
for a while
and discover yourself,
for when you are all alone
you know who you are.*

*Then steady yourself with surety
of what you discovered about you,
and when you interact with others again,*

## FRIENDS | FAMILY

*you will know
who is who.*

## PAGE OF PENTACLES

*Did you know, dear ♋ signs,
that you can live your best life
when you share it
with those you trust most?*

*It is easy as a water sign
to believe that you should
please everyone you can,
for it is you who cares about
how everyone feels.
But take into consideration
who **you** truly trust,
and those are the friends and family
to give your attention.*

*We know to you it sounds quite harsh,
but caring most for those you trust
will ensure you are cared for as well.*

FRIENDS | FAMILY

## OAK

*Did you know, dear ♋ friends,
that with just one gesture,
you can cause a change in plans?*

*If you happen to see a relationship fade away,
you can decide whether to pursue it
or go a different way.*

*There is no harm in moving on
if you feel compelled to,
so let go when you feel it is time to.*

*Not everyone you meet is
meant to accompany you
throughout your whole lifetime.*

♋

## MOON

*Do you trust me, dear ♋ signs?*

*For as you see me in the sky
waxing and waning
through time,
growing and receding.*

*This too
is what you must do
to conserve your energy.*

*Do not expect yourself to show up
bright and shining
each and every day,
for you need rest and reprieve.*

*Know that even with this inconsistency,
your dearest friends and family
will understand this,
if you tell them it is what you need.*

FRIENDS | FAMILY

## MOST TREASURED TAKEAWAYS

- Letting go of attachments to the past and enmeshments with others not only allows them to succeed, but frees you as well.
- When you allow your family to grow and expand into who they are becoming, you give them the greatest gift you could offer them.
- You are never solely the one to care for another. Release some of your burdens, by sending them an angel for assistance.
- Think of how close you are to your loved ones and imagine how all of humanity is one big family. When we realize we are one, hate will be erased.
- When you let go of sending love and care to others from a place of obligation, your heart expands and opens.
- Ask Archangel Lavender to assist you in clearing and cleansing the connections between you and your loved ones, because even when these relationships are difficult, they still fill your heart.
- When you take time to retreat from everyone else, you connect with your true self and can come back to your interactions with more clarity and surety.
- It is okay to give more attention and care to those you can trust rather than spending your valuable love on every single person you are somewhat connected to.

♋

- Decide which friends and family members you wish to stay connected to and which ones you are ready to move on from. Not all relationships are meant to last a lifetime.
- The moon is not consistently there every day as the sun shines, yet you still trust her. You ♋ signs, are the same way. You need time for yourself. Just tell your friends and family when you need alone time.

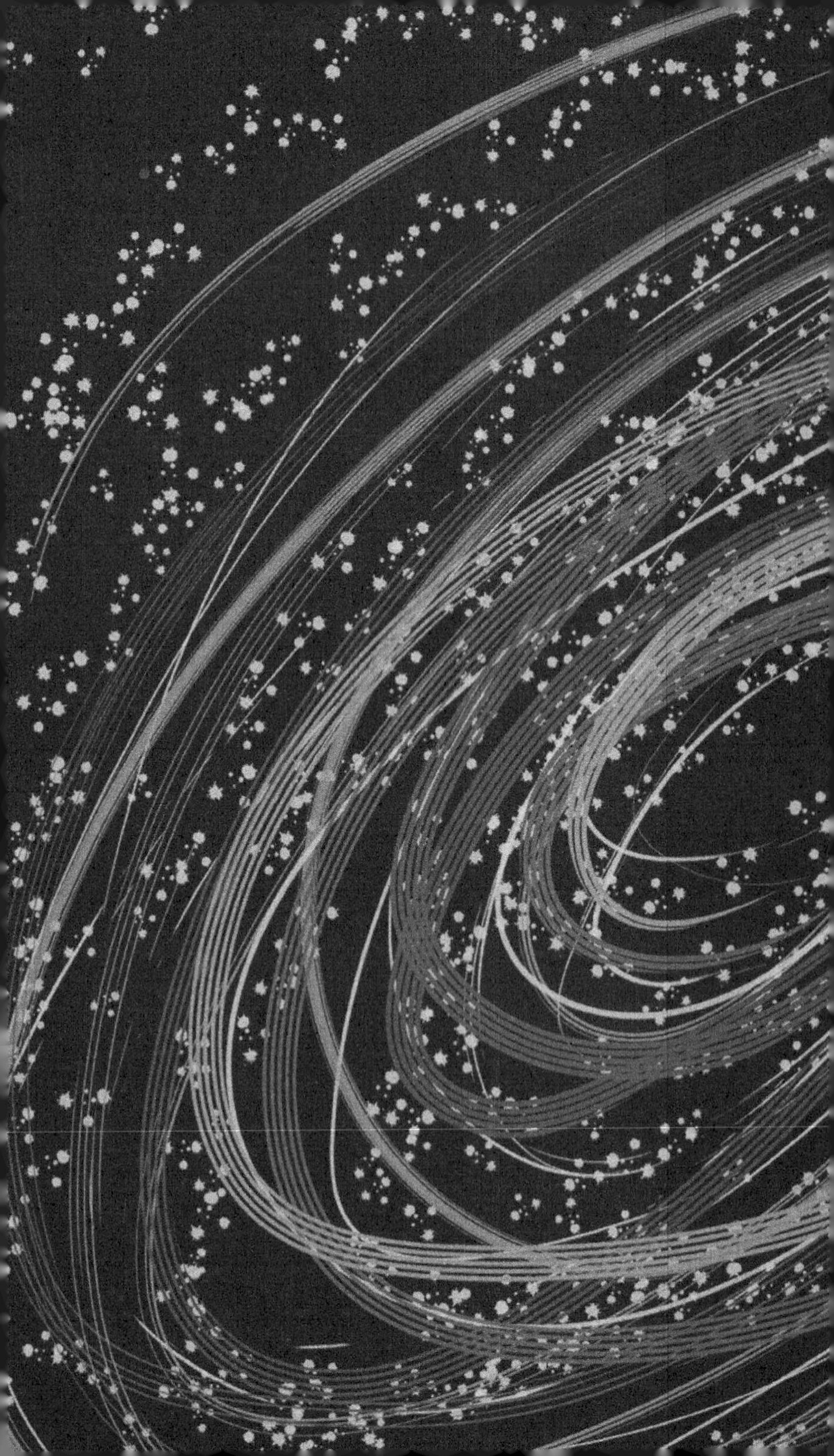

# HOW CAN ♋ NURTURE A FUN AND FULFILLING LIFE?

♋

## CRAB

*What a joy, dear ♋ signs, it is for you
to see how loved you are,
regardless of how carefully
you attend to others.*

*Our suggestion to you
is to take a solo retreat.
Find a place you can pamper yourself
without worrying about what others need.*

*It is keen of you to care, for sure,
but this comes
quite naturally to you.
Rather than thinking of how to give,
see how you can return
to you.*

## LAPIS LAZULI

*What makes you happy, dear ♋ signs?*

*This is a question on some of your minds.
For it is easy to feel happy
when all things are smoothly running,
but when things are more dreary,
what do you do then?*

*The answer lies within,
for no matter
what circumstance you are in,
you can find those feelings easily.*

*Just make sure that you also feel
the more challenging ones as well,
for if they well up inside you,
they will certainly overflow.*

*So, move through the emotions
as they arise and always come back
to the security of lapping happiness.*

♋

## ISIS

*Dearest ♋ signs, why are you so sad?*

*There is something in your past
that has been haunting you,
and although many of you
may not think of it on a conscious level,
it may be holding you back
from feeling the fulfillment you desire.*

*Letting go of this is exactly
what you need to do.
So, first find out what it is
(either you know already
or can find a hypnotist),
and once you see it you can feel it
from a place of compassion.
And once you acknowledge it,
you can allow it
to fade into oblivion.*

HAPPINESS | FUN

## ANSUZ - ANNA'S ANCESTOR GUIDES

*When was the last time, dearies,*
*that you decided*
*to do something just for you?*

*Perhaps for some of you,*
*it was today,*
*and for others, you may not*
*even recall the last time.*

*The happiness you gain*
*from caring for others is great,*
*and when it's married*
*with the care of yourself,*
*it will feel like you are the most blessed.*

*So, celebrate the times when you*
*are amongst your mates*
*but also know that when you are alone,*
*you can create that feeling*
*of wholeness as well.*

♋

## NYMPHS

*Have you ever seen a fountain, dear ♋ signs?*
*Think of it often in regard to your life.*

*For instance, when there is a pond*
*with a fountain in the center,*
*the water circulates and*
*is spouted up in all directions.*
*When it comes back down, it creates ripples.*

*This is how you can make*
*your life more fun, too.*
*What you can do*
*is to carefully pool your energy*
*and then circulate it all around.*
*That is, when you are feeling down,*
*gather your energy just like a reservoir.*
*Then circulate it around*
*by doing something fun for you—*
*by creating something new,*
*dancing, baking a cake,*
*or coming up with a list of recipes.*

*Whatever it is, your energy*
*will expand into a new realm,*
*and when it is done,*
*you will feel the happiness ripple out.*

HAPPINESS | FUN

## ARCHANGEL LAVENDER

*Dear ♋ souls,*
*it is I, Archangel Lavender,*
*here to assist you on living*
*with more fun and happiness.*

*First, dear ones, think very carefully*
*about what it is you want,*
*for quite often you are concerned*
*with providing others*
*with what they want and need—*
*that you neglect what you truly wish to be.*

*Assessment of your needs and desires*
*will bring up an awareness*
*that allows you to see*
*how your wants may be completely different*
*from what you've been doing.*

♋

## YARROW

*We have told you already,
dear ♋ signs,
how necessary it is for you to,
yes, bask in the Moon,
but learn to find the Sun
again and again
with each passing day,
for in your times of darkness,
the light begins to fade.*

*It is most important for you
to find the light within
and know that you can
find a secure and steady light inside
to take with you in the dark of night.*

*Your happiness
depends on it!*

## PAGE OF PENTACLES

*Oh ♋ signs, let me tell you
how fun your life could be
if you allowed those emotions
to set you free.*

*It is easier than it sounds.
You thought your emotions
were dragging you down,
but when you become
aware of them most regularly,
you see that they can be
loved and nourished fully.*

*For when you acknowledge
how you feel
and let your body respond,
you are able to heal
and find the fun
and fulfillment you desire.*

## OAK

*Did you know, dear ♋ friends,
that winter is when
you can still have fun.*

*Hear me out.
The storms of winter are coming soon,
and the winter cold is upon you,
but think of how much fun it can be
when you lay dormant for a while.*

*You, dear friends,
have an inclination for this
more than some other signs.*

*When you are cozily snuggled up
away from the hustle and bustle,
the best days are upon you.*

*So even if going out
seems most fun for others,
think of how you can play
on those winter days.*

## MOON

*Dear ♋ signs,
do you have the slightest idea
of how it is to be fully seen?*

*Think about when you are truly glowing
and determine what it is you are showing.*

*When you know
what makes you glow,
you see what
makes life worth living.*

## MOST TREASURED TAKEAWAYS

- When you take a solo retreat to pamper yourself, you will discover more of yourself.
- When you move through all of the emotions you have, even the challenging ones, you can come back to a steady lull of happy ones.
- There may be something from your past that is keeping you from feeling happiness. Determine what it is, and when you acknowledge it, it will fade away. Then, you'll get your happiness back.
- You do not need others to feel happiness. Know that when you do something just for you, it can make you feel just as wonderful.
- Do something that fills you with energy. Make something that will not only provide you with fun in the process but will expand the fun after it is done.
- Take special time to tune in to what you really want without regard for what others need or are asking your assistance for. It might be completely different than what you are spending your time on.
- Develop your light within by finding the Sun each and every day. These practices will assist you when darkness closes in. Your happiness depends on it.
- When you acknowledge the emotions that are more difficult, you will heal and find in your heart the ones that bring you the fun and fulfillment.

## HAPPINESS | FUN

- What is fun for you? Others might see it as going out, but for you, your happiest times might be snuggling up on days when you are stuck inside.
- What lights you up? What makes you glow? When you know that, you know what makes life worth living!

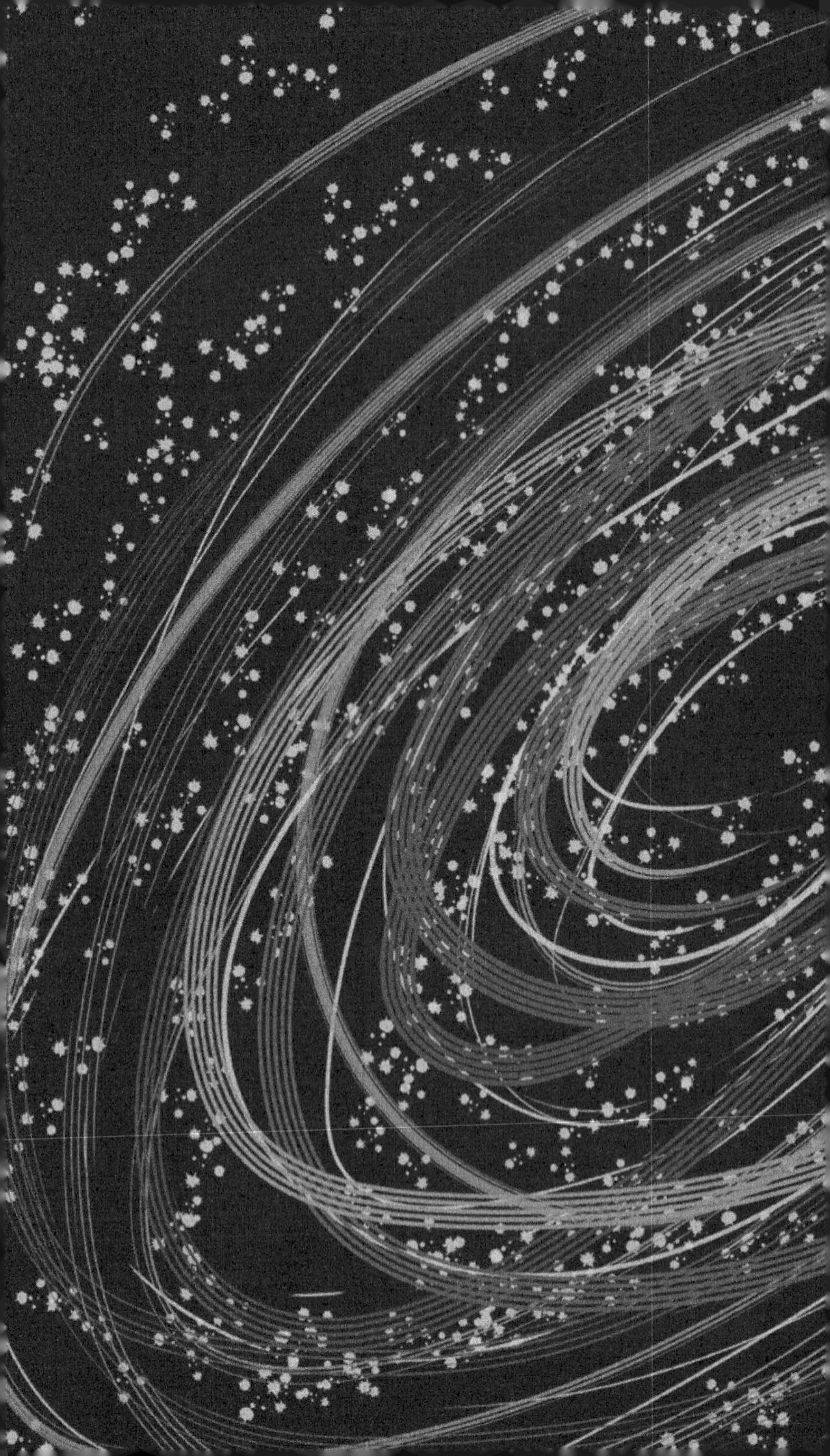

# HOW CAN ♋ ORIGINATE A HOME THEY LOVE?

♋

## CRAB

*We know, dear ♋ signs,
how important home is to you,
for you love to spend time
cuddled and cozy in your own space
with all your loved ones surrounding you.*

*However, it is necessary for you to see
how we, crab animal spirits,
hold our home wherever we go.*

*How can you sense
that your shell of security
is always with you
no matter where you are?*

## LAPIS LAZULI

*Oh, dear ♋ signs,*
*what a place you live in.*

*The state of your home*
*mirrors your emotions,*
*so make sure to tighten the faucets*
*and keep your dishes clean,*
*for even the most well-kept home*
*has its disasters every once in a while.*

*Be sure to fix them as they arise*
*to your awareness,*
*and no problem will be too big to handle*
*if you address it promptly.*

♋

## ISIS

*Now listen carefully dearest ♋ signs,
your home is a special place,
as it holds all you find dear to you,
but listen very carefully.
Not all is as it seems.*

*The things you possess
are not what makes it.
But rather the energy it holds.*

*So, spend time often
clearing and cleaning
each and every place,
and when you do,
your home will truly become
your sacred space.*

# HOME

## ANSUZ – ANNA'S ANCESTOR GUIDES

*Worthwhile is your time, dearies,*
*when you spend it on your home,*
*for when you create*
*a space that feels cozy and warm,*
*you make something that you will enjoy*
*each and every day.*

♋

## NYMPHS

*What is it you need, dear ♋ signs?*
*Although others may not recognize*
*how you may need more of a shell than others,*
*you can tell them so.*

*Do not determine your requirements for a home*
*based on what others tell you!*

*For instance, if you need a place*
*of more structure and soundness than others,*
*make it be known.*

*You require a place of shelter,*
*like a crab needs its shell,*
*a peaceful place you can retreat to,*
*to be completely left alone.*

*For when the tides get rough and the sea swells,*
*you will have a place to feel comfortable.*

# HOME

## ARCHANGEL LAVENDER

*Hello, dear ♋ souls,*
*it is I, Archangel Lavender,*
*here to assist you*
*on creating a home you love.*

*Listen carefully, for home is very important to you.*

*When you go about your day,*
*imagine what you do*
*and how your space*
*can be more conducive to you.*

*For instance, dear ones,*
*your kitchen may be the place*
*you spend lots of time in.*
*Is it providing you with what you need?*
*If not, imagine how it would look*
*if it fulfilled its purpose with more comfort.*
*The same goes for all the rooms*
*you spend time in.*

*How would they be if they*
*gave you the feeling of comfort?*

*When you have a picture of this in your mind,*
*continue to think of it often*

♋

*with ease and happiness.*

*Then, in divine time, it will be so,
if it is truly meant to be.*

# HOME

## YARROW

*Oh, dear ♋ signs,*
*do you love your home?*

*If not, learn very quickly*
*how to change that around.*

*For your home is a place*
*where you reside*
*that gives you steady reprieve*
*from the busyness of your day.*

*But when you learn to cultivate that safety*
*no matter where you are,*
*you will know that you are home*
*no matter where you are.*

*And learning to love yourself*
*is the only thing you*
*must attend to.*

♋

## PAGE OF PENTACLES

*I wish to say, dear ♋ signs,*
*that even though you regard your home*
*with much importance,*
*it is even more likely that you*
*love what it represents.*

*Allow me to explain to you what it is I mean.*

*There once was an old lady*
*who lived in a shoe,*
*and she knew exactly what to do,*
*because she was stepping forward constantly,*
*and never drifting away from the Earth.*

*I know this is a silly take*
*but think about what it means for you.*

*Your home represents stability and safety,*
*comfort and snuggly feelings.*

*If you understand that those are the feelings*
*you most want, it doesn't matter*
*if your home is in a shoe or a boat.* [18]

---

[18] I believe that this is a reference to either (or both) the "old woman who lived in a shoe" or the "old lady who swallowed a fly." Both are nursery rhymes. The former about a woman who has so

# HOME

## OAK

*We want to tell you, dear ♋ friends,
something that won't be comfortable for you to hear,
but in knowing it you will be able to let go of fear.*

*The steadiness you seek
in having a stable home
is not always possible.*

*There are times
when you need to move,
times when your
home life needs adjustment,
times when you
cannot rely on your family
to see you through.*

*During these times,*

---

many children she doesn't know what to do, so she whips them and sends them to bed. The latter about a woman who accidently swallows a fly and tries to solve the issue by swallowing other creatures but ends up making things much worse. Both women are overwhelmed and do not handle their situations gracefully. The Page of Pentacles, however, knows a very capable and grounded woman, who is not even slightly disturbed by her external circumstances of living in a shoe (being crammed in a small space) or a boat (living with constant change and ungroundedness). I like the Page of Pentacles version the best. By the way, I had to Google these rhymes after I channeled this because I couldn't fully remember them. Turns out they were even more relevant than I would have guessed.

♋

*you feel ungrounded,
but listen to what you can do.*

*Instead of finding security from others,
or in your environment,
learn how to build strength
by standing on your own feet.*

*When you cannot rely on the outside
to bring you security,
know that within your own heart
lies the courage to feel at home
no matter what is going on.*

## MOON

*Ah, dear ♋ signs.*

*When you are truly home,
you will know it,
but it may not be what it seems.*

*Hear me out,
for although you may think
it will be four walls and a roof
with plenty of coziness inside,
this is not the truth,
for your home
resides inside.*

*It is not the material things,
but rather those that live in your heart.*

*Who and what do you find in your heart?
Take a vision trip to discover them.*

## MOST TREASURED TAKEAWAYS

- Although it feels wonderful to have surroundings that nourish you, consider building an energetic shell around yourself, so you feel secure no matter where you go.
- Your home reflects your emotions. For both, when you address issues quickly, no problem will be too big to handle.
- It is the energy of your home that makes it feel special. When you take time to cleanse and clear it, it will feel even better.
- It is time well spent when you create a home that is warm and cozy, because you can enjoy it each and every day.
- You may need a more peaceful place than others do, so speak up and say what you need in order to feel at ease even when there's a storm.
- Imagine all the rooms of your home in a way that would be conducive and comforting to you. If you do, you will manifest them in divine time if they are truly meant to be.
- Develop a sense of home within yourself by learning to love you no matter what.
- Develop your sense of security and safety within, and you will be at ease no matter what circumstances you are in.
- You cannot always rely on others to grant you security, so learn to cultivate it yourself. Your heart will show you the way.

# HOME

- It sounds cliché, but your home is in your heart. Rather than just nodding and moving on, take an inner journey to see for yourself.

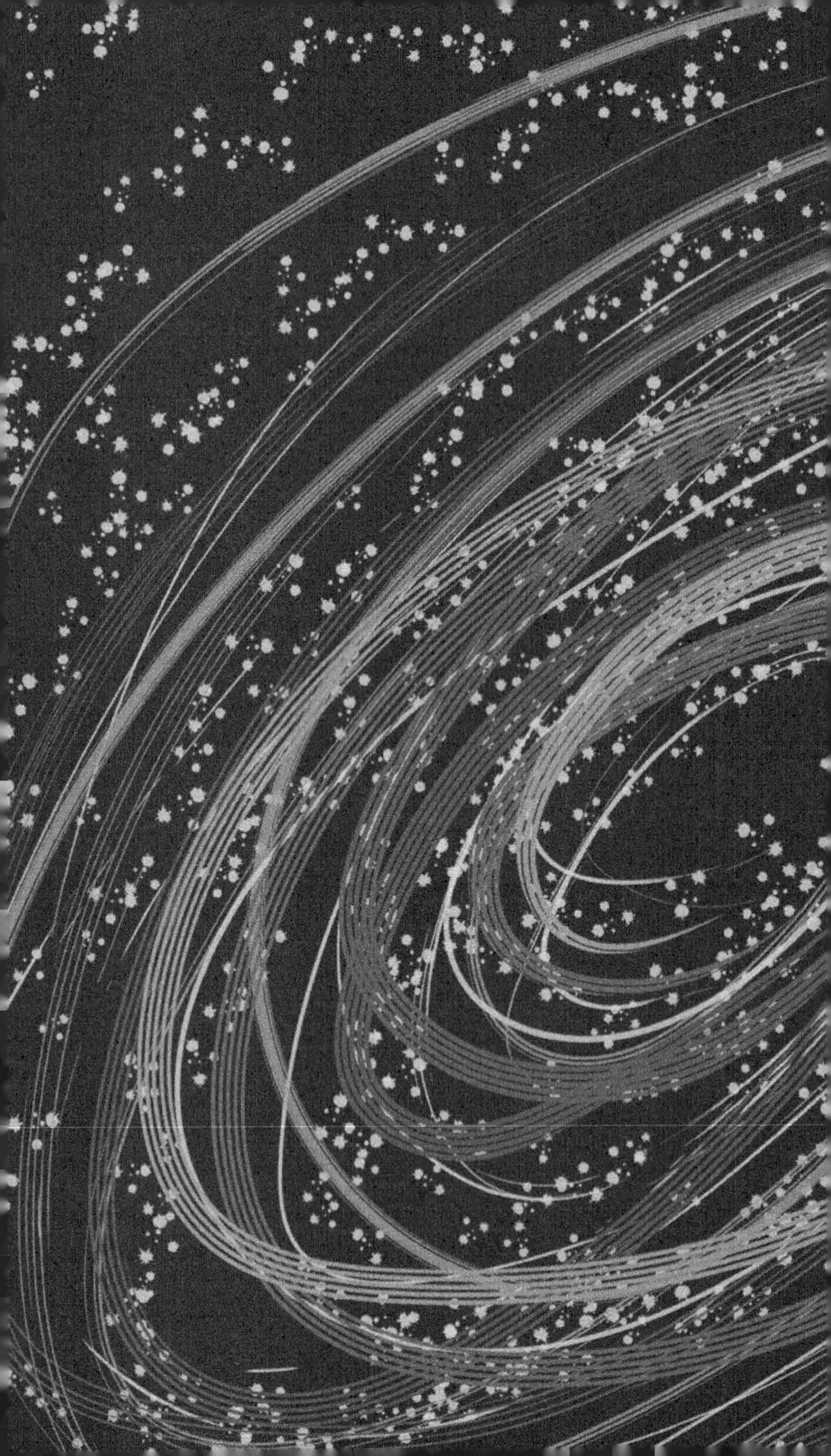

# HOW CAN ♋ ORIGINATE AND SUSTAIN WELLBEING?

♋

## CRAB

*First and foremost,
dear ♋ signs
take care of yourself!*

*As simple as this sounds,
it is not always easy.*

*You take care of you
in whatever way you need to,
and in the caring for yourself,
you set an example for all else!*

## LAPIS LAZULI

*Once or twice in your life
you've probably
had a scare, dear ♋ signs,
for your worries can magnify
when you let fears
override your mind.*

*Even when things seem dire,
they can be addressed
when you face them head on,
and you will find that
most often
things are not as bad as they seem.*

♋

## ISIS

*Your emotions, dear ♋ signs,*
*hold the keys to your health.*

*Even if you care for your body*
*and your mind with nourishment,*
*if your emotions are flooded*
*with worry or regret,*
*you will not heal completely.*

*So, take time to learn*
*how to release them in a healthy way,[19]*
*and your radiance will soon begin to shine.*

---

[19] EFT Tapping or Qi Gong shaking may be good avenues for you.

## ANSUZ - ANNA'S ANCESTORS

*Greet the day with thanks in your heart,
because when your life is waning,
you will see how each day was important!*

♋

## NYMPHS

*Did you know, dear ♋ signs,
that the flow of your qi is most necessary?*

*Imagine how your energy moves
when you are healthy.
When you keep from being stuck or stagnate,
then you will feel more at ease,
and your body will thank you.*

## ARCHANGEL LAVENDER

*Hello, dear ♋ souls,*
*it is I. Archangel Lavender,*
*here to assist you on living with health.*

*The most important thing for you,*
*dear ones, is to take care of yourself fully.*

*Now this is not as easy as it seems.*
*Some of you believe you are already doing so.*

*But think carefully of your needs*
*and the needs of your body.*
*Do you rest when you are tired?*
*Do you feel emotions as they come up?*
*Do you take yourself for a walk?*
*Do you change yourself*
*when you need refreshment?*
*Do you let go of unhealthy*
*attachments?*

*If the answer is yes to all these*
*and more questions like this,*
*then you are exactly as you need.*

*If not, how can you make that adjustment?*

♋

## YARROW

*Have you been seeping in
others' emotions again,
dear ♋ signs?*

*This is a huge thing for you to learn
how to manage,
for if you are always swaying
from your own emotions
to all others you know,
you will become very confused and tired
and begin to feel quite under-the-weather.*

*The most important thing
for you to learn from me
is that you must take care
of your energy!*

## PAGE OF PENTACLES

*What matters most for you
to get up and get going,
dear ♋ signs, is that you enjoy
whatever you do for exercise,
for finding motivation
is not easy for you
unless you see your workout
as something fun and
enjoyable to you.*

♋

## OAK

*Give up the need to comfort others
if it isn't conducive to you.*

*Think of all the times you
give your power away
by shutting down your authentic needs
if they don't match what others say.*

*When you allow yourself
to be swayed by everyone else,
you aren't able to stay well
and be true to yourself.*

## MOON

*Did you know, dear ♋ signs,*
*that when you*
*flow with my tides*
*you will see improvements.*

*As I wax and wane*
*so does your energy,*
*so when you go with that flow,*
*you will see how the brightest glow*
*comes only after*
*taking time to rest and reprieve.*

## MOST TREASURED TAKEAWAYS

- Although it is easier said than done, take care of yourself, first and foremost.
- Worries can cause illness to become worse than it actually is, so address issues as they come up if you want them to be easier.
- If you hold worry or regret, you won't find it easy to heal. Look into ways to heal your emotions in a positive way.
- When you grow older you will realize how each day is important, so be grateful for all of them.
- Learn how to allow your qi, lifeforce energy, to flow easily, and your body will naturally become healthier.
- Think carefully about all the ways that you can more fully nourish yourself and your body. Do you have room to grow in taking better care of you?
- Taking in other people's emotions can be confusing, tiring, and draining. If you learn to manage your energy, you will feel so much better.
- Finding an exercise that is enjoyable to you makes getting up and going so much easier.
- Putting others needs before your own is more damaging to your wellbeing than you may recognize. Learn to say no and set boundaries when you need to take care of you.
- Your energy waxes and wanes like the moon, and it is only when you give yourself time to

rest, that you will be able to fully feel your brightest.

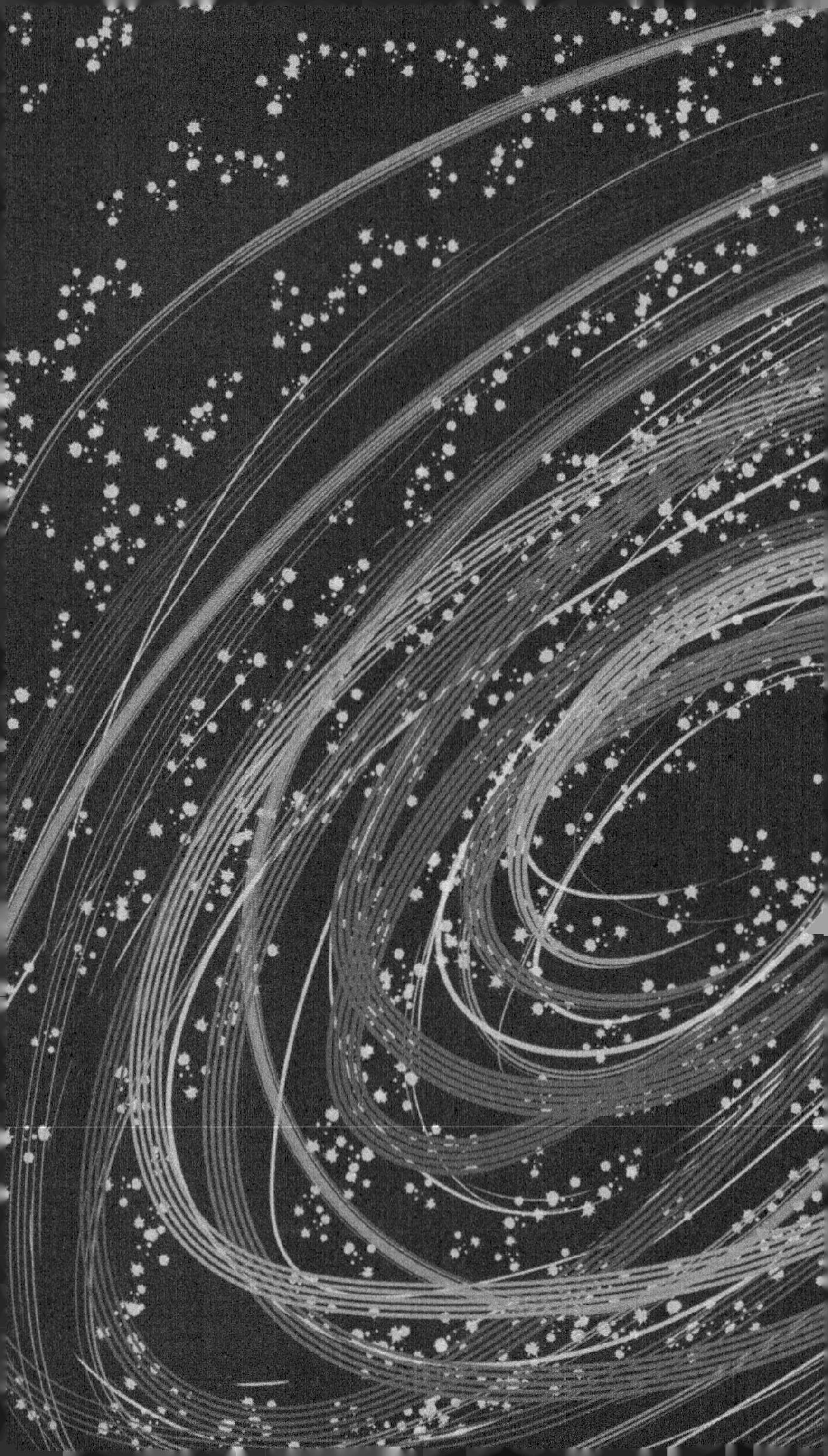

# HOW CAN ♋ NURTURE A SPIRITUALLY FULFILLING LIFE?

♋

## CRAB

*Once there was a star,*
*dear ♋ signs,*
*in our constellation*
*that had grown dull.*

*She was worried so much*
*of how she would be*
*perceived by others.*

*"What would the other stars think*
*when they saw my fading light?"*
*And as she wondered this,*
*her light began*
*to fade even more,*
*rather than focusing on*
*what she needed to strengthen her light.*

*This is something commonly occurring*
*in ♋ signs as well,*
*and before you get too worried,*
*we will tell you the remedy.*

*The truth, dear ♋ signs,*
*is that no one really was concerned*
*about the star's fading light,*
*for they were all focused upon*

## SPIRITUALITY

*their own brightness.*

*Once our dear fading star realized this,
she began to relax.
She opened up her shell,
and rather than being concerned
about what others would think,
she grew with her assuredness
that she did not need
to keep up appearances.*

*After shedding this shell
of fear of judgement,
she began to form a new one,
this time a shell
of powerful determination
to hold her own force
and protect herself
with the intention to be
secure in her sense of self.*

♋

## LAPIS LAZULI

*Take a look, dear ♋ signs,
with your mind's eye,
for there you will see with clarity
when you practice serenity.*

*The questions you have
are answered
with your inner sight
when you practice scrying.*

*Learn to open your mind
to what is possible for you
when you take time to view inside.*

## ISIS

*Listen, dearest ♋ signs,*
*for I have another story for you,*
*although this one is not like the other.*

*Once upon a time in a land not far from yours,*
*but rather in another dimension,*
*lived a little mermaid who sang in the sea*
*whenever she felt inspired to.*

*She was joyous each time the waves*
*became big and strong,*
*for it reminded her of her father.*

*She was happiest when the water*
*sparkled in the sunlight,*
*for it reminded her of her mother.*

*The way the ocean welled her eyes*
*when she thought of those she loved most*
*was how she remembered that all are connected.*

*For even though her mother and father*
*were no longer around,*
*she recognized them in the elementals*
*who were all around her.*

♋

*Even those, dear ♋ signs,*
*who seem far away*
*are only a thought and feeling away.*

SPIRITUALITY

## ANSUZ - ANNA'S ANCESTOR GUIDES

*Once there was a raft
upon the open sea, dearies,
and although it was quite sturdy,
it was full of holes,
for the logs were roped together
with gaps betwixt them.*

*This is how your soul is.
Instead of worrying about being perfect,
know that you still can
go atop the water,
sailing along with enough buoyancy
to not be drowned in the depths.*

♋

## NYMPHS

*While you receive the energy of your Spirit,
dear ♋ signs, you will always feel alive.*

*Your Spirit holds your body
and even though it is
necessary for you to be healthy,
not everyone is aware of it,
but without it, you would be dead.*

*Think of it this way.
The water is on the Earth in the oceans,
and although you think of the Earth
as made of dirt and clay,
it would not exist without
the abundance of water around it.*

*So, take some time to ponder this
and recognize how important it is
to nourish your Spirit.*

SPIRITUALITY

## ARCHANGEL LAVENDER

*Dear ♋ souls,
it is I, Archangel Lavender,
here to help you connect more with your Spirit.*

*Listen, although you are living in a body now,
your Spirit is really what is fueling you.*

*When you feel like something is not right,
the Spirit part of you is not fully connected to you.*

*So, learn how to invite it in.*

*This can be a simple practice
of noticing when
you are feeling down
and taking some alone time
to call your Spirit in.*

*When you do so,
you will be living more aligned
and will feel more like yourself.*

♋

## YARROW

*Your Spirit manifests
inside of you,
dear ♋ signs.*

*Your intuition is strong,
and your soul is
always seeking
more security and safety.*

*So, learn to receive
from your Spirit
whatever your soul needs,
and in doing this,
you discover
you are exactly what you need.*

## PAGE OF PENTACLES

*You, dear ♋ signs,*
*know of a rope*
*as a single thing,*
*but when you look closely*
*it is many pieces of twine*
*braided together*
*forming one lengthy thing.*

*You too, can imagine then*
*how your life is—*
*a single thread*
*braided with many others*
*to create a lengthy existence.*

*You see, your soul is one*
*of many extensions,*
*and your lifetime is*
*only a single rendition*
*of many iterations.*

*It is necessary for you to see*
*because viewing the other*
*parts of the rope*
*will help you untangle*
*the emotions of your soul*

♋

*Knowing this will assist you
to feel whole.*[20]

---

[20] This is talking about viewing the parallel timelines of your soul extensions, which can be done through hypnosis or meditation. Healing those parts of you will help you untangle your emotions.

## OAK

*One day, dear ♋ friends,*
*the sky will bring down rain,*
*and on another it will shine*
*the light of the Sun.*

*Just because there are*
*clouds now does not mean*
*you've done anything wrong.*

*Sometimes the rain is needed*
*in order to appreciate the Sun.*

*When you learn the lesson you need to*
*in order to become a stronger version of you,*
*the rain and clouds will drift away,*
*and the Sun will shine upon you.*

♋

## MOON

*Dear ♋ signs,*
*I tell you time and time again*
*that the flow of the seasons*
*is significant,*
*for you especially,*
*and it is true*
*with each rendition of existence.*

*For just as there is death and decay*
*with each waning moon,*
*there is in each and every life form.*

*It is not something to fear,*
*for the dark moon births a new moon.*

*So too is your existence*
*as the All and ever*
*part of the whole.*
*So, get used to the cycle,*
*and when it's your time to go,*
*you will know*
*it is never ending.*

# SPIRITUALITY

## MOST TREASURED TAKEAWAYS

- When you let go of the obligation to keep up appearances, you allow yourself to shine brighter than you imagined.
- When you take the time to practice scrying, you will see all that is possible for you.
- No matter how far away you are from those you love in the material world, when you sense the presence of them in your surroundings, you are reminded of how we are all connected.
- Think of your soul as a raft. It does not need to be perfect as long as it has the buoyancy to stay atop the water.
- Think of your Spirit to your body as the oceans, rivers, and streams are to the Earth. This will illustrate how vital it is to nourish your Spirit and for us to have healthy oceans.
- Your Spirit can give you extra energy if you take time alone to call it in. You'll feel more like you if you do.
- Your own Spirit can nourish your soul in exactly the way it needs. In that sense you already have exactly what your soul longs for.
- Your current lifetime is only a single strand of the entwined existence of your soul. When you heal the others, you'll heal your current reality as well.
- You may be going through a spiritual initiation. Whatever difficultly you are having is something

♋

to learn from. Once you clear it, you will feel the Sun.

- Get used to the cycle of the Moon, for it echoes throughout the All with each and every life and throughout all of existence.

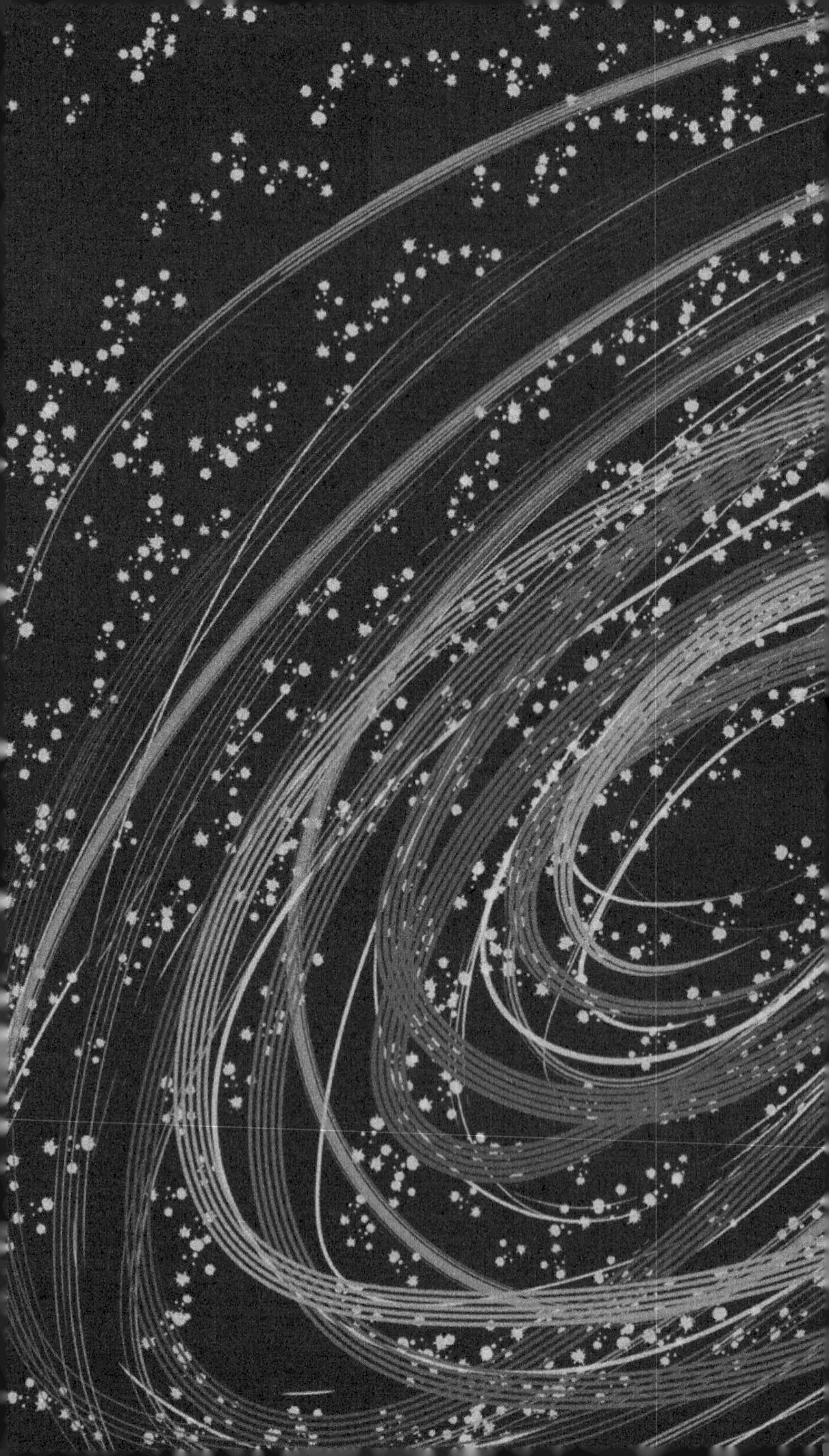

# HOW CAN ♋ NURTURE A SIGNIFICANT CREATIVE LIFE?

♋

## CRAB

*Oh, dear ♋ signs,
we want to tell you
that your creativity is such a value.
Not necessarily for others
but for you.*

*When you create from your soul,
you connect with
the deeper part of you.
The part of you who
longs to feel received.*

*When you see that aspect
of yourself that wants to be held
above all else,
you hold him/her/them most
when you follow
the flow of creativity.*

# CREATIVITY

## LAPIS LAZULI

*Oh dear ♋ signs,*
*your creativity shines*
*when you set aside time*
*to let it flourish.*
*For some of you may scrapbook,*
*and others of you may decorate,*
*but no matter what*
*your medium is,*
*you have the power to create,*
*so do not let this inclination*
*sink to the bottom of your list,*
*for it is as important*
*as expressing what you wish.*

♋

## ISIS

*Once, dear ♋ signs,
there was a toad
who lived upon the land,
and he was very keen,
for he understood
that creating was more
about energy than effort.*

*He did lots of sitting and pondering,
hopping only when he knew
exactly what to do
and where to go.*

*This way, his energy was high,
and so were the toadstools he designed,
for they were imagined with his mind,
and then pondered about
with a fluid understanding
of how much delight they would bring him
and any who sat upon them.*

CREATIVITY

## ANSUZ - ANNA'S ANCESTOR GUIDES

*Once more, dearies,
we wish to tell you that
when you create
from the place of security within,
your life will be magnificent.*

*How do you do this, you ask?
Well, first build a reserve
for when life gives you struggles.*

*Develop patience, clarity, and surety,
and when the floods come
you will still stand strong,
like a home with a foundation
upon a rock far above the high tide.*

*If you create your existence from that place,
your worries will dissolve.*

♋

## NYMPHS

*Wow, dear ♋ signs,
you are so blessed,
because your creative nature
is inherent.*

*The crafts that you make
or the pillows you sew,
the icing on your cake,
or the rainbows in your dreamcatcher—
each thing you create has
the capacity to change your temperature
from cold to warm.*

*You need this climate control
to live a life worthwhile.*

# CREATIVITY

## ARCHANGEL LAVENDER

*Dear ♋ souls,*
*it is I, Archangel Lavender,*
*here to assist you in*
*creating with more intention.*

*Creativity is a vast topic,*
*so I will be narrowing it down,*
*dear ones, to fit into a notion*
*that is best for you to start with.*

*First, dear ones, I wish to say*
*that your whole life is a creation,*
*so no matter what you do or say,*
*it is bringing more of that energy to you.*

*So when you feel connected to the past*
*and think of all the things that have happened,*
*ask yourself,*
*is this what I want to continue?*

*If it is not, then learn to clear your mind of it*
*and absolve your emotions around it.*
*When you do that you will create from a clear slate,*
*and new prospects will come to you.*

♋

## YARROW

*Dear ♋ signs,*
*how creative are you?*

*I do love to tell you*
*that when you are*
*nourishing your creativity,*
*you are taking care of you,*
*for it is a deep part of you.*

*Learn to say no to others*
*whenever you feel*
*especially drawn to have creative time,*
*and in taking this time for yourself,*
*you will be renewed and ready for more.*

## CREATIVITY

## PAGE OF PENTACLES

*When was the last time
you went out for an adventure,
dear ♋ signs?*

*We know it is not usually
your creative ideal,
for you think instead
of making knick-knacks
or using watercolors.*

*Rather than seeing things you make
as your creative outlet,
think of how each day
is your creative pallet.*

*What colors will you choose today
as you create your day?*

♋

## OAK

*Your strength, dear ♋ friends,
is not within what you make,
but rather, inside of you.*

*Sometimes you have the notion
that whatever is outside of you
has the value.*

*But hear us now.*

*The truest strength lies within you,
because no matter what you do,
or what you make,
or what you create,
or whether you are able to or not,
you are worthwhile no matter what.*

*Have strength in your awareness
that you alone, are powerful.*

## CREATIVITY

**MOON**

*Dear ♋ signs,
you are most creative
when you express your emotions.*

*Rather than logically thinking
of how you can make
something worthwhile,
allow your emotions to guide you,
for when you set them free,
through expression most gracefully,
that is when your creativity
will be heightened
and your heart will lighten.*

## MOST TREASURED TAKEAWAYS

- When you think of your creativity as a way for you to feel held, you tune in to the deepest part of you, your soul.
- Taking time to do creative projects, no matter what they are, is just as important as expressing what you wish for. Both are ways to use your creativity.
- When you are very intentional about your energy, the actions you take are more meaningful. This is a way to better maintain your energy.
- When you develop the sense of security you need within, you will be able to create a life of magnificence.
- Using your creativity is an important way to nourish the innate nature of your soul.
- You are constantly creating your reality. When you keep thinking of the past, ask yourself if you want to continue manifesting that. Clear and cleanse your mind and emotional state to allow in new energies.
- Taking time for your creativity when you feel inspired is a way for you to take care and nourish the deepest part of you.
- Think of your whole life as a creative outlet. What colors are you going to paint with today?
- Nothing outside of you proves your value. Sometimes it is best to separate yourself from

# CREATIVITY

your creations and know that your inherent worth is there no matter what.
- Allow your emotions to assist you in your creativity. This will set them free in a most graceful way. In this practice, your heart will lighten.

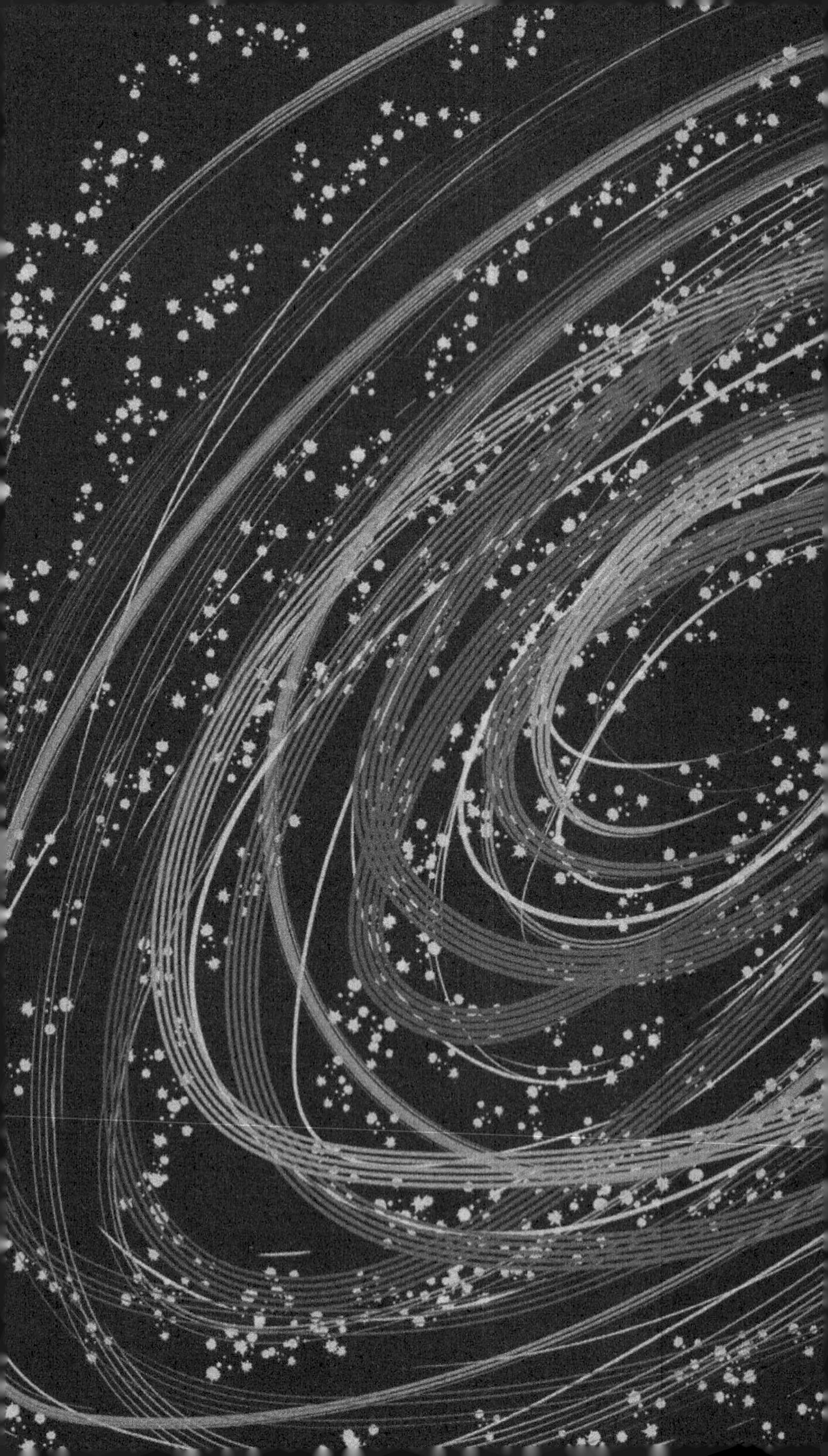

# WHAT MESSAGE ARE ♋ SIGNS MEANT TO HEAR EACH YEAR?

## CRAB

*Another year of your life is done,
dear ♋ signs,
and another is about to start.*

*Think of all you have done
to become more of yourself.*

*You alone are able
to create the life you desire,
so rather than dwelling on the past
think instead of how you can
build the strength to hold your own
in the sea of change
and on the land of shifting sand.*

## BIRTHDAY MESSAGE

## LAPIS LAZULI

*Dear ♋ signs,*
*Happy Birthday to you,*
*for as you turn one year older*
*you deepen your sentiment.*

*Another year of memories,*
*some good and some challenging,*
*each worthy of your recognition,*
*each elaborate in sensation.*

*Regardless of what you have experienced,*
*it is necessary for you to also look ahead*
*towards what is coming to you.*

*Careful not to live in the past, for you have*
*So much to look forward to!*

♋

## ISIS

*Dearest ♋ signs,
Happiest Birthday to you!*

*When you come to understand
how special you are,
you realize that all your effort
to be helpful and caring
was not the point of it all,
but rather a way for you
to understand and know
that you are just as significant
as all the rest.*

*So, take this day to pamper yourself,
and set an intention to do so more
throughout the entire year.*

*That is all dearest ♋ signs,
I wish you all the best
and want to remind you
to call on me, Isis,
whenever you feel compelled to.*

## BIRTHDAY MESSAGE

## ANSUZ - ANNA'S ANCESTOR GUIDES

*Happy Birthday, dearies!*

*You know quite well*
*that the older you get*
*the wiser you become,*
*but do not forget*
*that wisdom can also come*
*from those who are*
*quite a bit younger than you,*
*for they remembered better than you.*

♋

## NYMPHS

*Happy Birthday, dear ♋ signs!*
*One two three*
*four five six seven eight,*
*no matter how*
*many years you are,*
*you are never too old*
*to have some fun.*

*So take this day to celebrate*
*in a way that is true to you*
*and do whatever you want*
*regardless of what anyone says to you.*

BIRTHDAY MESSAGE

## ARCHANGEL LAVENDER

*Dear ♋ souls, Happy Birthday!*

*It is I, Archangel Lavender,*
*here to assist you in your coming year.*

*Listen, dear ones, the new year comes*
*with the Sun in the sky shining upon you,*
*whether it is covered by clouds,*
*that is up to you.*

*You may have had days*
*that are filled with sadness and rain,*
*but when you understand*
*that beyond that is brightness*
*always there to bring you vitality,*
*you can more easily decide*
*to let the darkness go*
*and step into your lightness.*

*That is all dear ones.*
*I wish you all the love for you to receive*
*and give you many blessings.*
*Take care and have a blessed year.*

## YARROW

*One is two*
*when another year*
*is added on*
*and so forth*
*and so on.*

*As you can see,*
*dear ♋ signs,*
*another year is added in,*
*and you may feel resentment*
*for the number*
*you've just become,*
*but learn to let that go,*
*along with all the other things*
*that have kept you*
*from fully stepping*
*into your present reality.*

BIRTHDAY MESSAGE

## PAGE OF PENTACLES

*Happy Birthday, dear ♋ signs,*
*we are so very proud of you,*
*for on this day, you became.*

*It is not always an easy thing to do,*
*for a soul is hard to stuff into a body.*

*But listen very carefully now,*
*for what I say next is the most important.*

*On that day, the day of your birth,*
*you said yes to being on Earth,*
*so remember that today,*
*many years later,*
*and remind yourself again*
*how being here is worth it*
*despite whatever has happened.*

♋

**OAK**

*Happy Birthday, dear ♋ friends!*

*When you acknowledge
all you have done this past year,
thinking of all you've learned,
take note of what you can do
to live more aligned with you.*

*Stand straight and tall,
for when you pride yourself
on who you are
others will be able to lean on you
without you toppling over.*

## BIRTHDAY MESSAGE

# MOON

*Once, years ago,
dear ♋ signs,
you were a babe
small and new.*

*This life you
have sown
has been fruitful
on many levels.*

*Think back to
all your blessings,
and know, dear ones,
that the time of
the year for reflection
is upon you
for when you reflect
on what has been
you will see
what is worth
growing towards.*

## MOST TREASURED TAKEAWAYS

- Crab spirit animal invites you to briefly think of all the ways you have grown stronger in your Self this past year, but also imagine how you can build even more sense of Self in the coming year.
- Lapis Lazuli invites you to acknowledge all you have experienced in the past year, but make sure you look ahead to what is coming to you!
- When you discover that the point of your nurturing nature is to understand that you are just as significant as all the others, you come to a new level of consciousness. Ask Isis for assistance.
- Wisdom comes with age, but don't forget that young ones have the wisdom of remembering.
- No matter how old you are, take some time to have some fun, in whatever way you want to!
- Your birthday can be a brand new beginning if you decide to let go of past sadness and know that the Sun is shining his brightness upon you.
- Let go of any resentment you feel for being the age that you are now, as well as all the thoughts and feelings that are keeping you from enjoying the present moment.
- At the moment of your birth, you said yes to being on Earth. Remember this and know it is still true to this day, no matter what you have gone through.

# BIRTHDAY MESSAGE

- When you learn to live more aligned to your true nature, your soul and your Spirit, your strength will make you more capable of caring for others in the way you wish to.
- Reflect on all the blessings you have had in order to know what is worth growing towards in your new cycle.

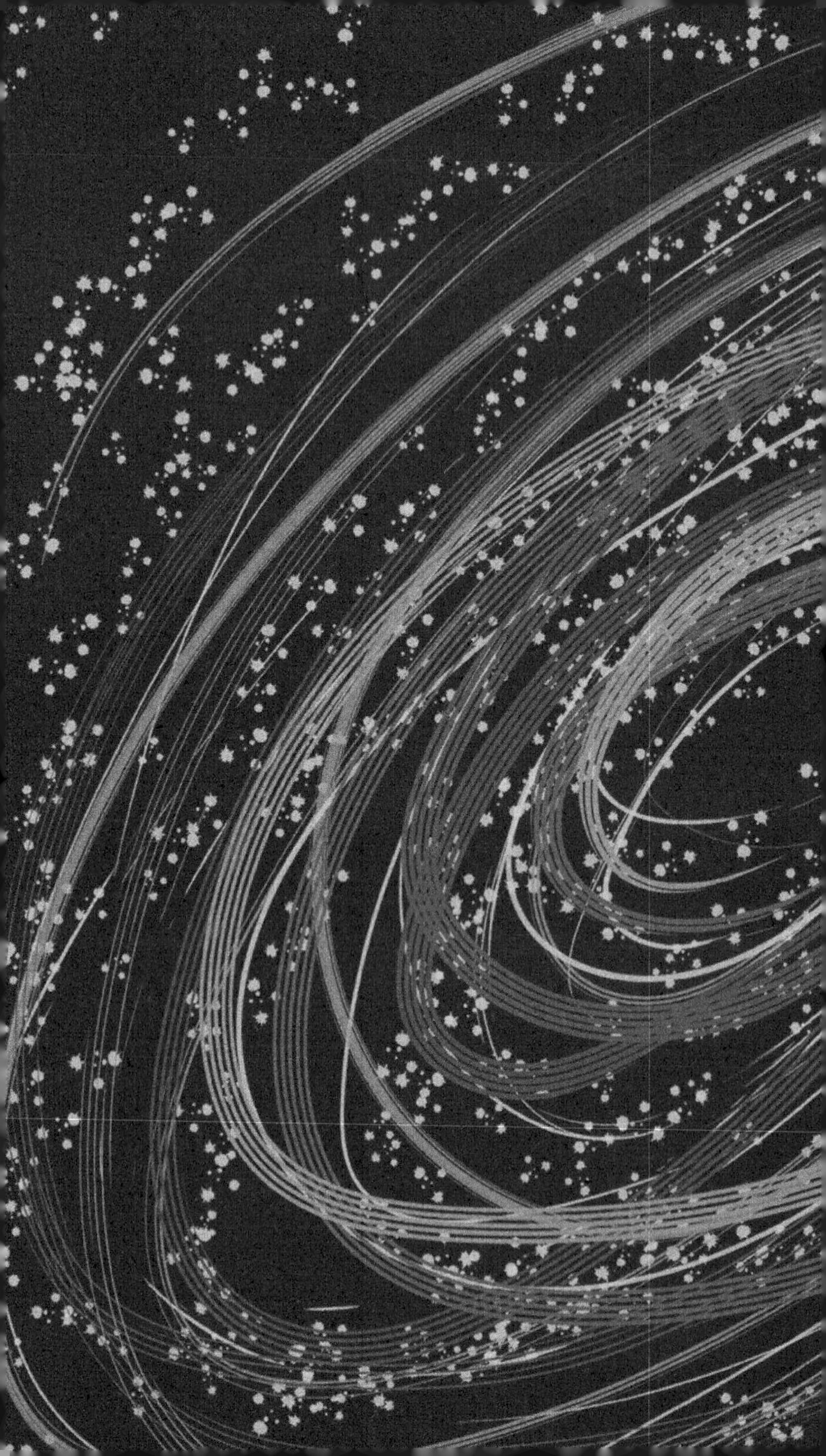

## AND WHERE IT REALLY BEGINS . . .

♋

## CONCLUSION

These nurturing sentiments from your sign's spirit guides have been a delight to transmit to you! I hope they inspire you to live a life that not only is more balanced but is also more meaningful and fulfilling!

As you have heard, your innate care, nourishment, emotional intelligence and intuition are so important to tap into, but it is up to you to make sure you feed yourself first, so you can truly make a difference in the lives of others. Showing up for yourself means flowing with your energy levels so you can fully embody your Spirit.

This book contains the reflective surface of support for you to live a life more aligned with your soul purpose, but now it is up to you. Will it be something you just read and find delight in? Or will it also be a significant key to continually ride the waves to live your best life? I have faith in you! Go soak up your soul's journey, affectionate and caring ♋!

As you have likely recognized, each spirit guide has their own personality just as you do. Even though ♋ signs share similar traits, each one of you uniquely embodies your own significance and individuality. Be more of you, and you will feel more whole.

This spirit guide resource only scratches the surface of showing what assistance is available to you from the spirit realm. For each of you not only has these ten guides but also a whole host of ones specifically there to help you along your journey on Earth. Although sometimes you

# WHERE IT REALLY BEGINS

may want to go it alone, know that regardless, you have endless support.

♋

# RESOURCES

### More for ♋ Signs

For a free resource page purely devoted to ♋ signs with more channeled messages from guides, meditations, and tools to connect with spirit, register at

www.annaswansun.com/courses/cancer

### Video Resources

For stories and spirit readings, messages from celestial beings, and meditations to balance the elements subscribe to Anna Swansun's YouTube channel. @annaswansun

### Book Resources

Receive messages for your Sun, Moon, Rising, North Node, Planets in Domicile, and Stellium signs in Anna's other books:

*Aries: Bold Insights from Your Sign's Spirit Guides*

(Published at the Aries Full Moon: October 2022)

*Taurus: Rich Encouragement from Your Sign's Spirit Guides*

(Full Moon in Taurus: November 2022)

*Gemini: Witty Verse from Your Sign's Spirit Guides*

(Full Moon in Gemini: December 2022)

*Leo: Bright Inspiration from Your Sign's Spirit Guides*

(Full Moon in Leo: February 2023)

*Virgo: Helpful Ideals from Your Sign's Spirit Guides*
(Full Moon in Virgo: March 2023)
*Libra: Harmonious Notions from Your Sign's Spirit Guides*
(Full Moon in Libra: April 2023)
*Scorpio: Powerful Revelations from Your Sign's Spirit Guides*
(Full Moon in Scorpio: May 2023)
*Sagittarius: Timeless Wisdom from Your Sign's Spirit Guides*
(Full Moon in Sagittarius: June 2023)
*Capricorn: Useful Principles from Your Sign's Spirit Guides*
(Full Moon in Capricorn: July 2023)
*Aquarius: Innovative Ideas from Your Sign's Spirit Guides*
(Full Moon in Aquarius: August 2023)
*Pisces: Mystical Perceptions from Your Sign's Spirit Guides*
(Full Moon in Pisces: August 2023)
*Soul's Journey through the Signs: Accompaniment to the Astrology Guidebooks Series* (late 2023)

**Astrology Resources**

Go to www.astro.com or www.astro.cafeastrology.com for a free birth chart.

To find out how to read your chart to figure out your sun, moon and rising signs, where your north node is, and whether you have a stellium or planet in domicile, visit

https://www.annaswansun.com/findyoursign/
to watch a video tutorial.

To learn more about Astrology find classes from Nadiya Shah and other astrologers at
www.synchronicityuniversity.com

**Connecting with Spirit**

To connect with your ancestors through an ancestral healing course with Bridget Nielsen go to
www.bridgetnielsen.com/ancestralcourse

My website www.annaswansun.com is full of many resources to connect with the sun, moon, stars and spirit in a myriad of ways including blog posts, videos, recordings, and bundles.

## REFERENCES & FURTHER READING

Anderson, Emily. *Crystals: How to Use their Powerful Energies*. London: Sirius, 2020.

Bartlett, Sarah. *The Tarot Bible: The Definitive Guide to the Cards and Spreads*. New York: Sterling, 2006.

Cooper, Diana. *Archangel Oracle Card Guidebook*. Carlsbad, California: Hay House, 2021.

Forrest, Steven. *The Book of the Moon: Discovering Astrology's Lost Dimension*. Borrego Springs, CA: Seven Paws Press, 2010.

Gerrard, Katie. *Odin's Gateway: A Practical Guide to the Wisdom of the Runes Through Galdr, Sigils and Casting*. London: Avalonia, 2009.

Josie. *Materia Medica: Your Guide Through the Mystical Meanings of Plants*. St. Paul, MN: Tenderheart Studio, 2021.

Kindred, Glennie. *The Tree Ogham*. Derbyshire: Glennie Kindred, 1997.

MacGregor, Trish, and Phyllis Vega. *Power Tarot*. New York: Fireside, 1998.

Moorey, Teresa. *The Fairy Bible: The Definitive Guide to the World of Fairies*. New York: Sterling, 2008.

Morrison, Lori. *The Shaman's Guide to Power Animals*. Four Jaguars Press, 2019.

Shah, Nadiya. *Prayers to the Sky: To Know & To Love The Astrological Planets More Deeply*. Synchronicity Publications, 2020.

Thorsson, Edred. *Futhark: A Handbook of Rune Magic*. Newburyport, MA: Weiser Books, 2020.

Virtue, Doreen. *Ascended Masters Guidebook*. Carlsbad, California: Hay House Inc., 2007.

Wilkinson, Hugo, and Gill Pitts, ed. *The Tree Book: The Stories, Science, and History of Trees*. London: Dorling Kindersley Limited, 2022.

## ACKNOWLEDGEMENTS

I thank all my guides, guardian angels, the Archangels, Ascended Masters, gods, goddesses, divination tools, and nature spirits who have helped me write this book! Those who had their messages recorded as well as the ones who supported me with their energetic presence!

I thank Mercury and Uranus, because at the eve of their conjunction on April 18, 2022, I received the inspired idea for this book series!

I thank the Moon who provides encouragement and flow for me as I write this book!

Thank you to all my teachers, both human and non-human. I especially thank the Astrologers Nadiya Shah, Cameron Allen, Stormie Grace, Bracha Goldsmith, Michael Lutin, Nicole Garceau, and Marc Laurenson for their knowledge, inspiration, and wisdom.

Thank you to all the spiritual leaders who have guided, mentored, and facilitated my expansion. There are too many to name, but I want to especially thank Bridget Nielsen, Lee Harris, Ester Hicks, and Opheana & Sikaal!

I thank my husband Brandon for encouraging me to get out and be seen. I am grateful for his steadiness, acceptance, love, and support. I thank my cat, Tansy, who keeps me company while I write, she embodies a full expression of love and joy!

♋

Thank you, sensitive and devoted ♋ readers for supporting my work. Thank you for listening and following your inspiration to connect with me and your spirit guides!

Mystical Blessings!

## MORE ABOUT ANNA SWANSUN

Anna Swansun helps driven empaths and wandering starseeds feel their connection to the All by understanding their unique role within it and assisting them in creating a life of hope, balance, and fulfillment! Her clients and customers describe her as "warm," "caring," "delightful," "a pleasure and joy to work with," and full of "heart-based energy!"

She works closely with Spirit Guides, Angels, Archangels, Ascended Masters, Gods/Goddesses, Celestial Beings, Ancestors, Nature Spirits, and the Alu, a collective tribe from the Andromeda Galaxy. Anna brings messages to those who want to know more about the multiverse and in turn, themselves through her books, blog, and on her YouTube Channel. She provides guidance through astrology, channeling, and intuition to bring in wisdom from the stars and spirit to help people become more empowered, connected, and whole and to assist in creating the New Earth.

Just like you, Anna loves learning, expanding, and discovering more. She studied clairvoyance and psychic development under Astrid with the Moonstar Academy and completed Spiritual Life Coaching & Healing Practitioner Training at the Divine Light Academy. Anna participated in Bridget Nielsen's Ancestral Healing Course. She studied the runes with Northern Shaman Jeremy RJ White. Anna has studied astrology under Nadiya Shah, Stormie Grace, Cameron Allen, Marc Laurenson and Michael Lutin. She continually engages in more learning as

♋

a member of ISAR (International Society for Astrological Research) and through Synchronicity University.

When Anna is not reading, writing, learning, connecting with spirit, and creating, she is exploring forests and day-tripping to the ocean, swimming and doing Qi Gong, hosting and writing letters, crocheting and crafting, meditating and spending quality time with her husband and cat.

Made in the USA
Middletown, DE
14 January 2023